STUDENT'S GUIDE TO SCIENCE FAIR PROJECTS
Step-by-Step
Using the Scientific Method

STUDENT'S GUIDE TO SCIENCE FAIR PROJECTS
Step-by-Step
Using the Scientific Method

Madeline D Binder, MSEd
MS Human Services Counseling

Copyright

Dedication
It is my pleasure to dedicate this book to my loving, supportive family - my children Mark and Marla, daughter-in-law Angela, son-in-law Mike, and grandchildren, Zack, Noah and Alexa.

Acknowledgments
I wish to express my appreciation to my cousin, Marsha Portnoy, who edited this book. To the teachers and students who have given inspiration and suggestions.

Books by Madeline Binder

The following books are all available here, on TpT (Teacher's Pay Teachers
https://tinyurl.com/yve7etcj

For Parents & Teachers

How To Build a Toy Train/Activity Table: DIY Easy-to-Do Wooden Table Plans
Teacher's Guide to Science Fair Projects: Using the Scientific Method
Teacher's Science Fair Guide to the Engineering Design Process
Proven Ways to Fund Classroom Science Supplies (Free download)

For Parents

How to Prepare Your Child to enter Kindergarten in the Fall
Tools to Prepare Your Child to Enter Preschool in the Fall
Proven Ways to Make Summer Parenting Easier: Parents, Grandparents & Caretakers
How to Prepare Your Child for Public School After Being Homeschooled
How to Help Your Child Enter Middle School in the Fall
How to Prepare Your Child for High School
How to Prepare Your Child to go to College
23 Tools for Traveling with Kids and Surviving

For Students

Student's Guide to Science Fair Projects: Using the Scientific Method   Grades 5-12
Student's Science Fair Guide: Using the Engineering Design Process   Grades 6-12
Best Kept Tips & Secrets: How to Succeed at the Science Fair (included in the Student's
  Guides)

Table of Contents

Before Your Begin

How to Use This Book
Letter "AF" on the Timeline

Sequential Order
The ideas in *Student's Guide to Science Fair Projects* are to be read in sequential order.
Step 1: Print the **Table of Contents (TOC)**. Use it as a guide and checklist.

Step 2: Look in the Student's Appendix, for a list of all **Printables**. Print 4 copies of the Bibliography printable and 1 copy of all the other printables. Place the printed pages in a folder.

Step 3: Leisurely read the book from beginning to end. This will give you the whole picture of the process.

Step 4: Read all the rules for your school's science fair. They take precedent over what is written in this book.

Step 5: After you have read the whole book, cover to cover, go back to the beginning of the book and work the process… step-by-step.

At the end of each section is an "**Outcomes Checklist**". (*Outcomes* are explained later.) Print each Checklist page. Do not move forward to the next section until you complete each outcome on each of the lists.

As you finish each section, make a check in the box on the **Complete Science Fair Project Checklist** that you printed.

Step 6: <u>After you have completed</u> your science fair project, put everything together for your science fair. Go back and check off each section using a different color in pen or pencil.

Outcomes for this Book
Know how to decide upon a project that will keep you interested and enthusiastic throughout your science fair project.

Know the 6-Steps of the Scientific Method.

Know how to complete a long-term project from beginning to end.

Be armed with extra tidbits from the  to give you a winning edge.

Links in the Book
There are 2 kinds of links.
1. Amazon.com shortened links: http://amzn.to/1GCHYHg.
2. TinyURL links: this program shortens the links so they will be easy to copy.
3. All links have been checked personally by me and are safe.

Overview for this Section of the Book
WOW! Your teacher announced that your school is going to have a science fair and students are responsible for exhibiting their project. What did you feel? Enthusiastic? Despondent? Dreadful? Fearful? Excited?

Whatever you are feeling now, don't worry because this book is designed to walk you through the world of science fair projects, step-by-step. Yes, this book is for YOU! Follow the pages, one at a time. Take time, when suggested, so you do not get overwhelmed.

You may be thinking that not everyone likes doing a science fair project. I understand. A student can't like every subject or assignment. BUT a science fair project is a MUST at your school. What is the secret of enjoying this assignment?

 #1

Choose a subject that you love!

Another secret is to imagine you are a detective. Search for clues to solve the mystery of doing a science fair project.

In the Student's Appendix there are over 201 questions that you can consider. Scattered throughout the book are a few science fair ideas, topics, projects, motivational quotes, and helpful clues.

If you haven't been to a science fair you are in for a big surprise. It is a really fun and exciting event. In the Student's Appendix you can see what a science fair looks like.

Remember to watch for the **SECRET FILES**.

Your first motivational quote...
Success is a Journey – Ben Sweetland

Good luck and enjoy the process.

A Winning Science Fair Strategy
SECRET FILES #2

Every idea begins with your attitude and thoughts.
What you believe will happen, will happen.
Principle of Quantum Physics

Before you conceive of what you want to do for a project, let's read a story. It is a metaphor. What is a metaphor? It is where you take one idea and use it for another idea.

Let's say you are going on a vacation to Disney World. Does your enjoyment come only after you arrive? Not by any means. Your joy comes the moment you and your family decide to take the trip. As you look at the descriptive brochures you feel a thrill of anticipation even before the journey starts. Then you begin to visualize yourself participating in all the fun-filled activities.

Are you starting to get excited?
Let's read on . . .

Does the enjoyment end when your vacation is over? Not a bit. You'll have the pleasure of telling your friends of your experience, looking at the photos you took, and reminiscing about all the fun you had.

Can you imagine the feeling of accomplishment once you see your project come alive in photographs and videos after the fair?

The same is true for the adventure of coming up with a Science Fair Project. The moment you say, "*I am going to think of an outstanding science fair project*," you have already begun your successful journey.

Here is a little understood fact. *You are a success the moment you start on the road to success*. You gain happiness after taking the first step towards success. Therefore, you do not have to wait until you determine which science fair project you are going to dream up, nor for the project to be completed before you are a success. You can be a success right now! IF you BELIEVE this is true, it will be true.

OK, are you ready to stop reading, and start doing? Let's follow the clues to find a science fair idea that is just right for YOU…

Now…this is usually where a really HARD question springs-to-mind:
WHAT are the best projects to do?

And there's really an EASY answer…
Choose the science project topic YOU LIKE – because with science projects it's THE DOING that really counts the most! Don't get anxious….get excited! Science fair projects are fun!

What do detectives do to solve a mystery?
Ask questions, look for clues and discover answers.
What do Detectives do when faced with challenges?
Believe THERE IS ALWAYS A WAY!

Science Fair Projects are about investigating and solving mysteries; exploring topics, brain-storming ideas, doing experiments to find answers to questions. AND about NEVER GIVING UP!!!

What is the Mystery that you are really, really, really interested in solving?

What clues will you turn up when you investigate your project?

What answers will you uncover when you solve the mystery of science fair projects? Are the answers what you suspected them to be?

Are you ready to begin your investigation? Here we go!

Timeline

Difference Between a Goal and an Outcome
Background Information for Timeline
Letter "AE" on the Timeline

 #3

A GOAL is something you are aiming for, something you would like to achieve.

AN OUTCOME IS SOMETHING THAT WILL ABSOLUTELY HAPPEN. An outcome is something that your brain believes you already achieved.

Why is the wording so important?
Because what we say determines how we feel. Feeling you have accomplished something helps to reduce fear, anxiety – and most important – gives you a positive feeling of pride in your achievement as if it already happened.

What is a Timeline?
A timeline is a simple, effective plan of action that outlines what you must do in order to meet your outcomes. It shows the dates and completion of each step of your project.

To produce consistent results, you must manage your activities. The timeline gives you the tool to manage your time, energy, focus, and talents so you can thoroughly enjoy doing your Project.

Why Bother with A Timeline?
> *Small step-by-step actions, consistently taken over a period of time, have a giant impact.* – Anthony Robbins

You must be able to manage your time and priorities because it takes 2 to 3 months to complete an excellent science fair project. You can have the best intentions (goals) to complete a project, but if you do not have a means of organizing yourself, time gets lost because of a failure to manage time and priorities. You could lose focus and direction.

A Science Fair Project requires specific step-by-step actions taken in a particular order. When the Judge(s) read your Science Log, look at your display board, and ask you questions about your project, they check to make sure that you have included every step of the process. You MUST KNOW the steps you took as well as the results... **KNOW this information like you know 1 + 1 = 2.**

How Do You Use the Timeline?
You will plot the **OUTCOMES** on the vertical line and their respective dates of completion.

Take the printed Directions and Timeline template from the folder.

After you have completed putting the dates on your Timeline, attach it to the inside cover of your Science Log.

Keep the Science Log in a safe place. It will hold all the secrets to your science fair project investigation.

Shopping List 1
Materials to Purchase
Letter "AD" on the Timeline

First read about the following materials before making a purchase. Detailed information follows on the next few pages.

1. **For Background Research and Bibliography Note Taking**
   1 pkg white, 4 pkgs each a different color, 6" x 8" lined or plain note cards
   https://amzn.to/1GCHYHg

2. Amazon has a **Science Log Notebooks**: https://amzn.to/2ADoDz1 .
   Before purchasing a science log, read about how to choose a Science Log on page 8

3. **Day-Timer** : https://www.daytimer.com
   I recommend the pocket size 2 page per day indexed style.

4. **Tabbed sections**: https://amzn.to/2Y0Cc4k
   Purchase 2 packages, 1 for the Science Log and 1 for the Project Report

Science Log
Be Diligent in Keeping Your Notes
Letter "AC" on the Timeline

Overview

For your investigation, you will need a ***NEW*** notebook in which you will take notes as you do your investigation. Everything you do for your project will be kept in this notebook as well as tracking your thoughts, feelings questions, research and experiments. Let's call this your **SCIENCE LOG**. Sometimes it is referred to as a science journal or lab notebook.

A Science Lab notebook is the single most valuable tool for any scientist, whether they are seasoned professionals with years of experience or students doing a project for the first time. The science notebook is a permanent record of all you've done to create and complete a science fair project.

During the course of your project there will be dozens of details to keep track of. That is the reason for keeping a daily record of your project. If you are diligent about documenting everything you do, think about, and what happens as a result of your activities, you won't have to worry about forgetting something later when you write your report.

Your teacher will expect you to hand in your Science Log with your report. When you enter a science fair you will be expected to display this Log on your table. The Judge will possibly go through the book an ask questions.

How to Choose Your Science Log

There are many kinds of science logs, ranging from official science lab notebooks to makeshift notebooks. The table below offers a summary of different types of notebooks. Click on the link in the left column to read about each lab book at Amazon.com.

Types of Lab Notebooks

Bound Composition Notebook: https://amzn.to/1GTNs0m
A bound spine (not spiral) is difficult to use because the pages do not lay flat. This makes it is difficult to write near the margins. Easy to find at most stores. Students K-Middle School

Official Laboratory Notebook: https://amzn.to/1GTNLIB
Excellent for science fairs because has an area for creating a table of contents and numbered pages for easy cross-referencing. Some notebooks include reference materials such as amino acid codon table, metric conversions and periodic table. High quality to withstand lots of handling. Students K-College

Duplicate Style Lab Notebook: https://amzn.to/1GTMy3O
These notebooks are a subset of the official lab notebooks but have carbonless duplicate sets. Great way to keep your original work and give copies to your teacher or research partner (if you are working on a team). Research Teams, K-College, Teachers

Electronic Notebooks
Findings: ttps://findingsapp.com/
Lab Archives: https://www.esciencenotebook.com/
Available by using software or an online tool. Easy to organize and share data with teammate or teacher. Both come with free versions. Check with your teacher before using one for your science fair. Students, Research Teams, K-College, Teachers

Home Made Notebook - There are sturdy notebooks with dividers already in the notebook. Make sure that the covers are sturdy and that the pages do not easily tear out of the notebook. Perforated pages tend to do that. Students K-Middle School

Setting Up Your Science Log
Overview
Your Science Log is a permanent record of all phases of your project. Take out your Science Log printable. It will help you to set up your Log. It will also act as a guide as you do your project, so keep it in the front pocket of the Science Log. Keep the printables in the front pocket of your Log.

Whether you use an ordinary composition book or an official Science Lab Notebook, there are guidelines you must follow to make sure your notebook stays organized. Organization is truly the key to a successful project.

A Science Log is an invaluable tool when doing your project. It is a permanent record of all phases of your project, from beginning to end. The information that you gather will be the basis of your Project Report.

This is where you can keep track of ideas, comments, problems and ideas for solving them, notes, random thoughts that occur over the weeks and months of the process. It keeps all the information organized in a single place. It tracks the history of your project in sequential order – from start to finish. Whoever reads your Log will be able to completely understand your project and how you came up with your solution. They will be able to follow your journey through all the steps and will be able to duplicate exactly what you did. So, keep it neat!

It will also be handed in to your teacher and be on display at science fairs you participant in along with your Project Report. Did you know that the Science Fair Judge can question everything that is in the notebook?

Recording Your Entries

- **Get into the habit of writing in your Science Log every day**. Put a date in front of each entry, even if the entry is only a few words. This helps you keep track of the sequence of events and observations during your project.

- **Put your name and either a phone number or email address on the inside front cover**. That way, if your notebook is misplaced or lost, the finder can more easily return it to you. You can also include the title of your project and the date, for future reference.

- **Use a non-smearing pen, and write carefully and legibly**. If you make an error, just draw a line through it and make the correction. Do not use an eraser or white out.

- **Number each page of your Log**—it will come in handy later as you write your report. Some students organize the sections according to the steps of the scientific method.

- **Date your entries**. It will help you to keep track of when you did your observations and procedures.

- Keep the entries in **sequential order**.

- **Do not leave any pages blank**. Do not go back and fill them in later. Your Science Log must be a record of your project every step of the way.

- **Do not remove pages from your log**. If a page is accidentally left blank, draw an X over it, but do not rip it out.

- **Leave an X in large empty spaces**.

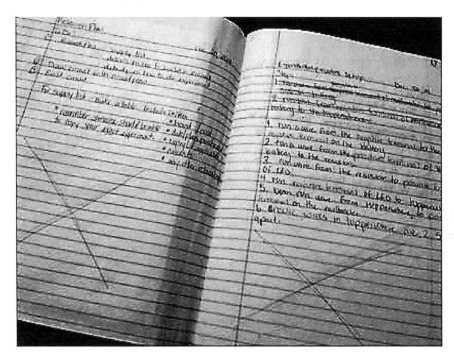

- **Make your entries brief**. Complete sentences are not required. Entries must have enough detail so that if you go over your notes a year later you will instantly understand the entry without wondering what you meant. Whoever reads your Log must be able to know exactly what you did.

- **Write legibly** so you or a stranger could read it. My cursive writing is terrible. To read what I wrote I need to print my notes by hand.

- **There cannot be any loose papers**. Glue (rubber cement if best), tape or staple any papers that need to be inserted in a particular place. For example, digital materials may need to be added to the Log. On the next page you can see loose pages that were taped to the Log. (see next page)

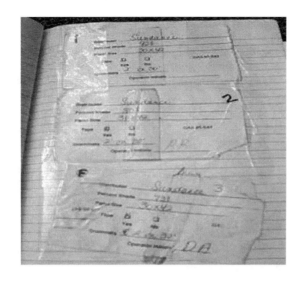

- Save a place at the front of your notebook for the **TOC**, which you will create later, as you gather your data. Ask your teacher if you can **write on tabbed sections** within the notebook, each section using a different color tab.

   Here are suggested sections:
   Timeline
   Background Research
   Variable / Hypothesis
   Materials List
   Experiment
   Data and Results
   Data Analysis and Conclusion

- **Keep your notebook handy**, especially when you are working on your project, someplace other than home, and thinking about your project. Great ideas often come at odd moments. Sure, you can jot down a note on a scrap of paper, or try to remember the thought until you get the chance to write it in your notebook. But you won't have to worry about losing the paper or forgetting an important detail if you have the notebook with you at all times.

- Write down all thoughts that come to mind about the project.

- Note anything you need to look up later.

What to Include in Your Science Log
Everything! The more details, the better.

I know that I am repeating myself, but keeping accurate records that follow specific rules for entry is very important.

Since the Science Log begins at the very beginning of your science fair project, record and date all thoughts that come to mind about the project, and what you hope to find out.

Record the steps, one at a time with a detailed account of your project activities so you will be able to go back to a previous step whenever you need to. By keeping track with such a detailed account, you will find it easier to analyze your data and write your Project Report.

Remember to staple, glue (with rubber cement) or tape all worksheets, forms and other pieces of paper. Date each entry so you know what you used it for.

The most difficult thing about keeping a Science Log is remembering to use it at each and every point in your project. Later, you'll be very glad that you did.

- **Brainstorming**
  The brainstorming that led you to come up with your project idea in the first place.

- **You will want to list**:
  - Sources you'll use in your background research, including books, articles and personal interviews. (This list automatically gives you the bibliography section of your report.)

  - Phone numbers or email addresses of everyone you contacted about your project.

  - Materials you'll need to conduct your experiments. Include where to find them and an estimate of what they'll cost.

  - Your hypothesis, the variables you will test and measure.

  - All math calculations. Be careful to be accurate. Write all numbers, temperatures, measurements, calculations and other relevant data. If you use Excel or an electronic program, list the log dates and file names. Tape or staple the printed copies in your Science.

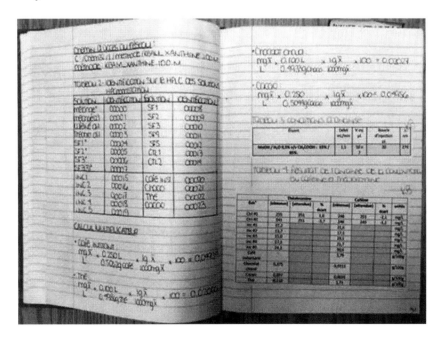

13

- Notes of all test measurements.

- o **You will want to describe in detail**:
  - Background research.
  - The experimental procedure - including your plans, any modifications you make, and any problems or mistakes you encounter.
  - How and when you set up your trials?
  - What were your results?
  - What worked and what didn't work?
  - What did you have to go back and re-do?
  - What insights did you have?
  - What conclusion can you draw from the data you've collected, including all measurements and calculations?

- o **You will want to create**
  - A log of activities related to your project.
  - Diagrams, charts, and/or drawings as a visual record of an aspect of your project.

Wilbur Wright's notes and drawings.

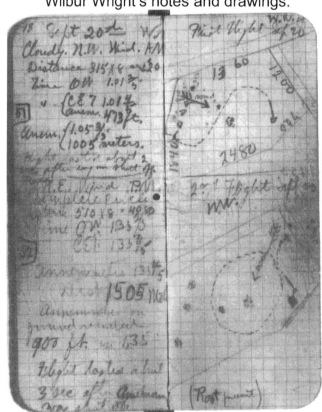

- Drawings or photographs of your lab setup or results of experiments (you can tape these into your Science Log).

- o **Remember to**
  - Put a date next to each entry.

- Keep the entries in sequential order.
- Write down any thoughts that come to you about the project.
- Make a note of everything you need to look at later.

With such a detailed account of your project activities, you will be able to go back to a previous step whenever you need to. And by keeping track with such a detailed account, you will find it easier to analyze your data and write your Project Report.

Sample of Note Taking in Lab Notebooks

Albert Einstein

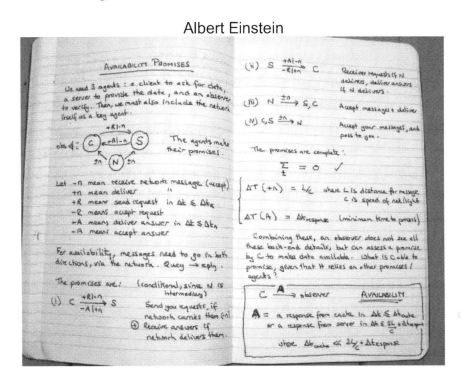

Student's Science Fair Logs

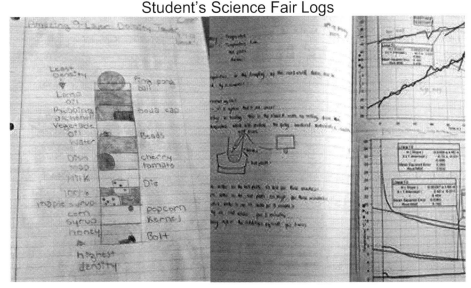

Day-Timer

When you know where you are going, you are halfway there.
Zig Ziglar

One of the habits of highly effective people is keeping a Day-Timer.

What fills your day? Attending school, doing homework, participating in school activities, meeting family responsibilities and having time for your social life as well as play time… and you may even have a part-time job! Just writing all of this makes me want to take a breath!

Juggling all these activities in your head is impossible, and can become stressful if you are not well organized on paper… not on your computer, iPad or cell phone. And now you are going to add to your busy schedule a time-consuming project. It is imperative that you remember to keep these appointments and be on time. I highly recommend that you purchase a Day-Timer.

True Story: I taught my son to use a Day-Timer in high school. When he was in law school and took out his Day-Timer® at the end of a job interview, the interviewer asked, "How long have you been using a Day-Timer®?" After a discussion about each of their use of a Day-Timer, the interviewer said to my son, "You're hired. Anyone who keeps a Day-Timer is someone I can count on!"

I recommend the Day-Timer® 2-Page-Per-Day Indexed Pocket Size Planner. It has room for notes, scheduled appointments and events according to the time of day.

Shopping List 1 Outcomes Checklist

Print this checklist, check the outcomes when they are completed, attach the form to your Science Log, and date your entry.

Did you accomplish your outcomes today? What's that? Your Timeline and Day-Timer, of course! This is *so-o-o* important. It will make a huge difference when you write your Project Report and Abstract. You will be thanking yourself because the tasks will go much faster than if you didn't.

Please be sure you mark ALL the steps and their respective dates on the timeline.

Check off the outcomes you accomplished.	✓
I printed and set up my Timeline.	
I purchased a Science Log.	
I set up my Science Log so it is ready to be used.	
I purchased a Day-Timer.	

After you check off all 4 of the outcomes, you are ready for the next section.

To be ready to discover among the many topics the one that's just right for you, read what we are going to do tomorrow. Then close the book and relax. See you tomorrow.

How Science Fair Judges Think
Tips for Doing a Science Fair Project

It is empowering to know what to expect from the Judges. Each school has their own criteria for judging, but here are some factors that judges most often look for when evaluating your project. Get inside the judge's mind.

1. **What do you do to ACE the interview?**

Judges walk from display to display, stopping at each one. Some briefly talk to every student and others take the time to do an in-depth interview. Don't panic, it only takes a couple of minutes.

Now is your opportunity to "show your stuff". You can use your display board as a prop, but the Judge wants to hear from you. Don't read from the display board. Use it to highlight your presentation by pointing to the charts, graphs and photos.
If English is a second language, take your time when expressing yourself.

o   Whatever your native language, talk in an easy, slow pace.

o   Clearly articulate your thoughts when you talk with the Judges. Do not mumble. Be confident.

2. **Be Prepared**
   When you have completed doing your science fair Project Report and Abstract, you must get prepared for your interview with the Judges. Being prepared will give you a winning edge.

- Write a brief two-to-five-minute talk summarizing your project. Talk about the theory behind it and why your project turned out the way it did. Your Abstract will summarize your project. Be sure to include the following:

  - How you came up with the idea.

  - A brief overview of how you did your experiment. Explain any terminology.

  - Your results and conclusion.

  - How your project contributes to others. Even if it will help a small population, your project is important.

  - The Judge will interrupt you to ask questions. You will not be able to tell them everything you know. But being prepared is what is most important.

  - On a 3"x5" note card, write some keywords to help you to remember what you want to tell the Judge(s). Bring this note card to the science fair. You will use it when you talk to the Judge who reviews your project.

- After you read **Questions Asked at the San Diego Science & Engineering Science Fair**, select a few questions that you think the Judges will ask you. Write the list of questions with their respective answers.

- Read and reread your background research. Know the facts as if you were studying for a school test.

- Practice your little "speech" and answers to your list of questions so you know them like you already know 2 + 2 =4.

- Practice telling others about your project as if they were the Judges: mom, dad, brother, sister, other family members, neighbor, friends, your pet.

- It is helpful to videotape yourself when you practice. Watch it so you can give yourself feedback. Keep in mind that you are just looking at feedback that helps you to improve.

SECRET FILES #4

It you get upset from what you see, just say to yourself,
I live in my actions, not my emotions.

- Be able to explain your graphs, tables, and theory behind your science fair experiment. Use your display board to point out diagrams and graphs.

- Make your explanation very simple so if a person does not know a thing about your project, they would understand what you say.

3. **Does your display board grab the Judges attention from 3 feet away?**
   The first thing the Judge sees is your display. It does not have to be flashy, but well organized.

4. **When the judge opens your notebook will it be well organized?**
   Does it have all the basic elements?
   - Daily notes that are dated.
   - Abstract
   - Research paper with bibliography, hypothesis, procedures, results - tables, figures and graphs

5. **Were you creative when doing your science fair project?**
   - Does your Big Question show creativity and originality?

   - Did you go about solving the problem in an original way? Did you give an analysis of the data for your science fair experiment? An interpretation of the data?

   - How about the type of equipment you used? Did you construct or design new equipment?

6. **Did you follow all 6-steps of the scientific method?**
   - Did you clearly state your problem?

   - Did you use scientific literature or only popular literature (newspapers, magazines, etc.), when doing your initial research?

   - Did you clearly state your variables?

   - Did you use controls? And if so, did you recognize their need and were they correctly used?

   - Does your data support your conclusions?

   - Do you recognize the limitations of the data / experiment? And did you state them in your conclusions?

   - Did you make suggestions as to what further research is warranted?

7. **Were you thorough in doing your science project?**
   - Did you carefully think out your science fair project, go about it systematically with well thought-out research following the scientific method?

   - Did you complete all parts of your research experiment?

   - Did you keep a Science Log?

   - Did you keep detailed and accurate notes in the Log?

8. **What was the quality of your technical skill?**
   o Did you have the required equipment to obtain your data?

   o Was the project performed at home, school, university or hospital laboratory?

   o Where did the equipment come from? Did you build it? Did you borrow it from somewhere? Did you work in a professional laboratory?

   o Did you do the project yourself or did you receive help? If you received help the judges are looking for you to give credit to those individuals.

9. **Did you have clarity with the details of your science project?**
   o Sometimes you may be asked to explain a short version of your project. This is where your abstract will be helpful. Look it over and become familiar with the information.

   o If a Judge asks what would happen if you changed a variable in your experiment, don't panic...you have plenty of knowledge in that computer brain of yours! On the spot, just create another hypothesis or idea about what you think will happen.

   o Are you familiar enough with the material to answer questions? Judges are not interested in memorized speeches or trivial details. They want to know what you learned.

   o Can you explain the purpose, procedure, and conclusions of your science project?

   o Does your written material, including your abstract, tables, charts and graphs, show that you understand your research project?

   o Is your material presented in an orderly manner?

   o Is the data of your project clearly stated?

   o Are the results of your project clearly stated?

   o Does your project display explain your science project?

10. **What are some questions that you may be asked?**
    Helpful Hints

    o What is most important when answering the Judge's questions is to be honest. If you don't know the answer, then be truthful.

    o Judges like spontaneous answers. Don't try to memorize answers. Know your stuff cold like you know 3 + 3 = 6. And you do, because you did the work! (Remember that computer brain of yours?)

- Know the formulas, terms and acronyms that you used for your science fair project. They may ask you to define some of the scientific jargon that you used.
- Science Fair Judges want you to succeed. They want you to shine. They are not trying to stump you or get you flustered.

- Either during your presentation or afterwards, the Judge will take notes. Don't panic! Many have to fill out a form for each project that they see. On that form are 5 areas (creativity, scientific thought, thoroughness, skill and clarity).

11. Glance over the **Judges Score Sheet** in the Appendix.

The Scientific Method vs. The Engineering Design Process

The Scientific Method – Scientists study things in the natural world to see how they work. They make observations about what they see, create hypotheses, and then design experiments that will either prove or refute them."

The Engineering Method – Engineers invent things that never existed before. They identify a problem and then follow the steps of a process that leads them to a possible solution. If the prototype does not work then they go back and refine, retest the prototype and / or brainstorm solutions, re-evaluate, and choose a different solution.

The Scientific Method | Engineering Design Process

Big Question → Gather Background Information → Identify Variables Formulate Hypothesis → Design Experiment Establish Procedure → Test Hypothesis by Doing an Experiment → Analyze Results & Draw Conclusions → Communicate Results

Define a Problem or Need → Gather Background Information → Establish Design Statement & Criteria → Prepare Preliminary Designs → Build and Test Prototype → Verify, Test & Redesign as Needed → Communicate Results

In either case, the experimenter / designer will find himself or herself going back and forth between steps. Working in this manner is called "iteration," and it is especially common during the final steps of the process.

The Scientific Method

Letter "AA" on the Timeline

This is a huge section of the book. It is the nitty-gritty phase of the investigation and therefore, very important. So... how do you stay focused? Well...

Bite by Bite!

Overview

Researchers do not have an outcome or solution in mind when they make their hypothesis. Their hypothesis is an educated guess. Whatever the findings turn up after their experiment is done, they say, "Oh, OK".

Now you know why science fair projects are so much fun! You are asked to do pure research. There is no right or wrong answer.

Q. What is the scientific method?
A. It is a series of steps that lead you from a question to an answer.

Q. How does it differ from the engineering design process?
A. Engineers create something new, whereas scientists study nature and how it works.

Q. What is the first step of the scientific method?
A. Observe something interesting in the natural world and formulate a question about it. This is called The Big Question

Q. What is the next step?
A. Do some research around the subject. – Do Background Research

Q. What is the third step?
A. Based on your research and observations, make an educated guess - Construct a Hypothesis.

Q. Is the fourth step to test the hypothesis?
A. Yes. You would do an experiment by which you change one element only. This is called a "fair" test.

Q. What is the next step?
A. Go through all your data, analyze it and then draw a conclusion.

Q. And the final step is…?
A. You must communicate the results of your experiment, either verifying or refuting the hypothesis.

Notice in the diagram below that the Scientific Method is really not a step-by-step process. Oftentimes a scientist rethinks what he believed and goes back to repeat steps to clarify his/her findings. A process that involves "backing up" is called an **iterative process**.

THE SCIENTIFIC METHOD

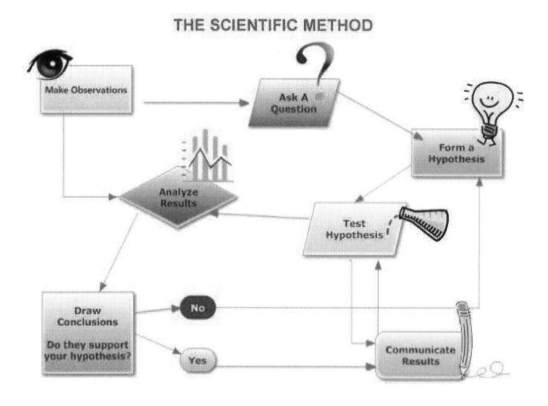

Details

The scientific method is a step-by-step process has been used worldwide for centuries. It is a **standardized process of experimentation** to explore observations and answer questions. It was developed over time since the ancient Greeks.

Aristotle (384–322 BCE) devised methods to try to find reliable knowledge based on observation.

Roger Bacon (1214–1294) was influenced by the writing of Muslim scientists. He chronicled the repeating cycle of observation, hypothesis, experimentation and verification.

Galileo (1564–1642) found the science of dynamics and is called the Father of the Scientific Method by The Encyclopedia Britannica (1970).

This process is used by scientists so they can replicate experiments and improve upon results by just changing one factor (variable). Through observation they are able to see how one change can **cause** a different **effect.**

Following the scientific method is important to you because you will have a step-by-step replicable process to follow that will help you to organize your science fair project. You may find a science experiment that another student did and just by changing one variable you can make it your own original project. That is what scientists do; they are constantly looking to make new discoveries.

Once you learn and experience the process you will be able to call upon it to make decisions throughout your life.

Topic Research
Letter "Z" on the Timeline

Do not begin this section until your Science Log is set up.

In the Student's Appendix, read **Science Fair Topics to Avoid** and **Reasons to Avoid a Topic**. No point in wasting time!

Before you step into doing the actual steps of the Scientific Method, you need to determine the topic that interests you. If you do not know the topic of your science fair project, then you need to do research what interests you. (Will explain how to do research later in the book.)

To determine the topic, first you must choose the science category because you will be required to register it when you enter your project in the science fair.

If you are planning on entering a top science fair, keep in mind that you must produce an original body of work (something that has never been done before). If this is your goal, then we suggest you work with a mentor in your science category and topic.

The next few pages will walk you through the steps of determining your category, subcategory and topic.

Choose a Science Category
Before Choosing a Topic
Letter "Z" on the Timeline

Finding the right idea for a science fair project can be challenging, especially if your teacher has not limited you to a specific area of inquiry. What your project will be depends upon what interests you, what puzzles you, or what you want to learn more about.

When you enter your school's science fair you will register your science category, subcategory and topic.

Great detectives follow their instincts. So...search your own mind for the answer to these questions:

What interests me most?
What do I enjoy learning about?

What thought first popped into your mind? Write it down in your Science Log.

If your response is, "I don't know," that's okay. Somewhere inside you is the answer. We'll stick together to find the category for your project by going through the following procedure together.

Let's read on. . .

We are going to go through an exercise to discover which subject category you *reeeally*, *reeeally* like the best. Look at the **Intel ISEF Category & Subcategory Science List** in the Appendix to help you to decide what field of science you want to focus on for your project. Print it and put it in front of you while you do the following process. It will lead you to solving this part of the mystery.

While looking at the list of categories, answer the following question over and over again:

Am I more interested in _____ or _____?

Write down the first thought that comes to your mind.

For example:
1) Am I more interested in…
Animal Science – study of animal life, their life cycle and animal interactions within their environment.

Or

Behavior and Social Science – study of the systematic analysis and investigation of humans and animals. Examples of behavioral sciences include psychology, psychobiology, criminology and cognitive science.

Make your choice now.

Not solved this part of the mystery yet? Let's continue… Let's say that you chose the category, animal science.

The next question to ask yourself is
2) Am I more interested in…Animal Science

Or

Biochemistry – the study of the chemical basis of processes occurring in living organisms, including how they react with each other and the environment.

Make a choice now.

3). Continue looking at the ISEF List; follow the process, until you find a category that excites you. Don't move on to the next clue until you complete the task!

4). In your Science Log write the category of science that you chose.

Category Selection Advisement

Many projects could easily fit into more than one category. We highly recommend that you review the entire list of categories before choosing the category that most accurately describes your project.

You don't need to compete in the same category as in your regional or state competition. Furthermore, most regional and state competitions do not use sub-categories. Most often Judges are matched to projects first at the sub-category level and then at the category level as best as possible, so still give the selection of a sub-category consideration. "Other" as a sub-category most often will match the project with a wide range of judges across the category.

Ask yourself the following questions to help in the selection of a category:

1. Who will be the most qualified to judge my project? What area of expertise is the most important for the judge to have? (For example, a medical background or an environmental science background?)

2. What is the emphasis of my project? What characteristic of my project is the most innovative, unique or important? (For example, is the application in medicine or agriculture? Is it inserting the proper gene or a method of farming certified organic vegetables?)

Subcategory of Your Category
Letter "Y" on the Timeline

The more we narrow down the possibilities, the closer we get to solve the mystery of your science fair project topic! So, let's narrow down the category to a subcategory.

Definition: A subcategory is a division of a category.

Let's say that you chose Plant Science.
Ask yourself, "What interests me most about plant science?
For example, would I enjoy learning more about *soil management* or *crop rotation*?

Look at the **ISEF Category & Subcategory** pages again.

Then take out your Science Log and write down this question:

What would be more fun to learn about, _____ or _____ ?

Keep on asking this question until you know that you have chosen the right subcategory that will *reeeally* hold your interest for a couple of months.

A sleuth keeps accurate records. Once you decide upon your subcategory, take out your Science Log, write down the process you just completed, and the category subcategory you are going to concentrate on for your science project.

Staple, glue or tape both the Category and Subcategory Lists in your Science Log.

Phew, I don't know about you, but I've got to get up and stretch.
You do the same...

OK, feel better? Then let's move on....

Choosing a Science Topic
Letter "X" on the Timeline

Anyone who has ever tackled a science fair project will tell you that the hardest part of the effort is finding a topic that interests you enough that you will gladly stick with it for the weeks (and sometimes months) it takes to complete the process.

What makes a great science fair project topic? One that *reeeally* holds your interest, involves you in a journey of discovery, and drives your curiosity. ... You will know what it is when you have a BIG grin on your face. And... your whole body moves up and down with a "YES".

Take out your Science Log and journal all the questions that arise from your readings, observations and discussions. The more questions you ask yourself about the world around you, the more you will be able to find the specific topic you will want to research for your project. Record every detailed step that you take as you do your inquiry.

Below are some ideas on how you can investigate to find your specific topic.

EXAMPLE 1: Let's say that you chose Plant Sciences as your category and the subcategory is Physiology. You know you chose this subcategory because you have an interest in how plant processes are affected by environmental factors. Now you need to narrow your topic to a very specific aspect of this subject.

EXAMPLE 2: Light is essential for the microscopic plant life (phytoplankton) that lives in the ocean. If you lowered a Secchi disk over the side of a virtual research vessel, could you discover how oceanographers determine the depth of light penetration? Then think about what science fair topic would interest you from this discussion. A question you may ask yourself is "How much light do microscopic plants need in order to live?" What experiment can you design to answer this question?

1st Option: Ask yourself questions:
> What makes me curious about _____?
> I wonder what would happen if _____?

2nd Option: What if nothing immediately piques your curiosity, don't worry. Sit down and let's go on an adventure to find what will be exciting for you to investigate. Honestly, you can do it! After all, this is the day you've been waiting for - the day you are going to narrow down your topic to a very specific area of interest.

3rd Option: Do a search in Google for science fair topic questions. For example, if you are interested in plants, search the keyword phrase: *science fair topics how plant processes are affected by environmental factors.*

4th Option: Read your local and school newspaper and school science book.

5th Option: Listen to adults' conversations.

6th Option: Talk to a scientist, doctor, your science teacher, parents. Ask them what piqued their curiosity in their field of study or expertise.

7th Option: Go to the library and read about your subcategory. There you will find encyclopedias, science fair books, science magazines, and other reference materials. Find out what aspect of this subject interests you the most?

Stick with your investigation and do not go any further in this book until you have your specific topic. This may take a couple of days.

1st Meeting with Your Teacher and Parent(s)
Letter "W" on the Timeline

It is important to get approval for your topic because there is no sense in doing research (which takes a lot of time) unless your teacher and a parent approve your topic. I know, it is your assignment, but your parents have to pay for the materials and your teacher has rules she has to follow too.

A science fair project is a HUGE undertaking and it is a group effort. You will need the support of both your teacher and parent(s). May as well have a cooperative attitude rather than bucking the system. Be honest, positive, enthusiastic and a good listener.

Before you meet with anyone, remember this: the secret of enrolling (influencing) someone is to be genuinely *ENTHUSIASM!* Radiate your smile from within!

Meet with your parent(s) first and explain that this is just a preliminary meeting. You will meet with them again after your teacher approves the topic and after you write your Big

Question and Hypothesis. Then you will have a more realistic view of the complete project.

Next, go see your teacher and tell her the same as you told your parent(s).

Do not move ahead to the next step unless you have approval by both parent(s) and teacher and complete the checklist.

Category, Subcategory & Topic Outcomes Checklist

Print this page, check off the outcomes, attach the form to the Science Log, and date your entry.

I accomplished my outcomes for this section because...	✓
I read, *How Do Science Fair Judges Think*.	
I determined the category of science.	
I decided upon the subcategory of science.	
I chose a specific topic.	
I met with a parent and my teacher. They both approved my topic.	

If you reached all 5 outcomes, jump up and down!!! You stuck with it. You accomplished a gigantic step today. Now you have found your perfect, "just right" topic. Congratulations! You laid the foundation.

Within a couple of days you'll build upon it. You now have your Science Project Topic.

Specific Help for Each Step of the Scientific Method
The following sections give you an **overview** of what you will do to implement and complete your science fair project.

The Big Question - The Scientific Method Begins by Asking a Question
What are you curious about? What interests you? What draws your attention? What have you seen that makes you wonder?

Your question will begin with one or more of the following words: How, What, Where, Which, Who or Why. A question that begins with the word, *what* will more readily help you come up with your hypothesis because it trances your brain to get to the unconscious truth.

Background Research & Ask an Expert
The library has now become your best friend because it has access to online research sites that are only available to those who pay a membership fee. These search programs are very expensive. Ask your school or public librarian to help you locate them.

Like other scientists before you, doing background research will save you a lot of time because you will not have to repeat mistakes that others made.

The Internet is another source of information. It does not always give you original research, which is what you need for your science fair project.

Forming a Hypothesis Includes **Variables** and **Hypothesis**
A hypothesis is an educated guess or prediction of what you think will happen. Write what you think is the answer to your Big Question or the reason for your observation. What makes this fun is there is no right or wrong answer!

Science Experiment - **What will you do to test your hypothesis?**
Your experiment tests whether your hypothesis is true, false or partially true. The experiment must be a *fair test*, which means that you only change one factor (variable) while all other factors stay constant (the same).

Allow enough time to repeat your experiments to ensure that your results are accurate and not an accident.

Data Analysis & Draw Conclusions
What did your experiment show?

When you have completed your experiment, it is time to collect your data and analyze it to see if it supported your hypothesis or contradicted it.

Like most scientists you may find that your hypothesis was false. What do scientists do then? Well, they create a new hypothesis and start the scientific method process once again. You <u>do not</u> have to do that for your science fair project.

If your hypothesis is true, it is a good idea to check and see if the results were accurate by repeating the process again exactly as you did it the 1st time.

Communicate Your Results
How to Write Your Report, **How to Write Your Abstract**, & **How to Make Your Display Board**

To complete your science fair project, you will communicate your results to others in a final report and/or a display board.

Professional scientists do almost exactly the same thing by publishing their final report in a scientific journal or by presenting their results on a poster at a scientific meeting.

I - The Big Question

Questions Lead to Answers
Letter "V" on the Timeline

Overview

Once you zero in on the general topic, it is time to ask the **specific scientific question** that will launch your science fair project.

o Begin your question with one of these words: how, who, where, why, which, what, when. Write the question in your Science Log.

Science Fair Question

Example: If you want to know if an apple grown with chemicals speeds up a person's pulse, your question may be, "When you eat an apple that was farmed with artificial chemicals, does it speed up a person's pulse rate?"

o Next, to answer the question, you must design what is known as a "fair test." In this test, you change one element (variable) but keep everything else the same. If you can't think of an element to change, go back and revise your question.

Example: When a chemically grown apple is eaten by a person does it increase a person's pulse opposed to when a person eats a certified organically grown apple?"

o You must also be able to provide some type of measurement—a number, a color, or some other trait—to show the results of your fair test.

o   Read your school's science fair rules to learn what tests are not allowed.

o   When you write your question, think about whether or not your project will need to be approved by a Scientific Review Committee (SRC). The committee is a group of at least three people that include a science teacher, physical scientist and biomedical scientist. They decide if your project meets the science fair's safety and legal requirements. They also make sure that all required forms are filled out properly.

    Some fairs have a committee called Institutional Review Board (IRB). They review proposals for projects that involve human beings to make sure that no harm can be done to the people in the study.

    The projects are approved before the experiment is done. Most fairs follow the **ISEF Rules and Guidelines** (https://tinyurl.com/y8nuchjj). The document is quite extensive. Take your time to read it. If necessary, take a couple of days. Particularly pay attention to Human Subjects (psychological surveys), Hazardous Substances and Devices, Nonhuman Vertebrae Animals, Potentially Hazardous Biological Agents.

o   Will you have time to perform 3 to 5 trials of your experiment?

Formulating Your Big Question

Focusing on the right question is key. The answer to the question is what your science fair project is all about. Ask yourself, "What is the question that is going to drive my project? What am I hoping to learn / discover?"

o   Your question must be on a topic that will keep your interest until you have found the answer.

o   It must be specific enough that you can find the answer with a simple experiment.

o   You must have between 3 and 5 sources of information so you can build on what others have explored.

o   The question must be focused and direct, and must begin with one of these words: what, when, which, why, where, who or how.

o   Think about what kind of experiment you could perform to answer your question.

o   You must arrange a "fair test" whereby you control all factors, keeping all conditions the same except for the one variable you are changing.

o   You must be able to use a number that represents a quantity such as length, width, height, percentage, energy, voltage, velocity, etc.

o   Before you begin, verify that your experiment will be safe to perform.

- You want to have all the equipment and supplies assembled before you conduct your experiment.

- Does your experiment meet all the rules of the science fair that you are entering?

What is an Excellent and Poor Big Question?
Let's define the terminology:

1. The Big Question is <u>not</u> your hypothesis.

2. There is a distinction between a science fair topic and the Big Question.
   - A science fair topic focuses on a general area of science that you are interested in: the weather, wind or solar energy, plant growth, organic foods, water microbes.

   - The Big Question narrows down your topic to something very specific or zeros in on a specific problem. The results are all measurable.

What is an Excellent Big Science Fair Question?
An excellent big question shows cause and effect. For instance, "How do fertilizers affect the pulse rate of a person?"

What was affected? Person's pulse rate
What caused the affect? Fertilizer

In the above example you can explore if there is a difference between chemical and organic fertilizers.

Another way to know if you wrote a good question is to determine if it is testable. Do you have a measurable outcome?

YES! A person's pulse rate can be measured before and after eating the apple that was fed chemical fertilizer.

Can you make a comparison to another variable that can be measured?

YES! You can compare a person's pulse rate after they eat a certified organic apple.

More Excellent Questions
- What produces more energy, wind or solar?
- How does the age of a shower head affect the growth of bacteria of the water sprayed?
- Where is the best place to plant your herbal garden?
- What freezes faster, cold water or hot water?
- Which type of cake flour makes the lightest cake?

Examples of Poor Questions

A question that does not have a particular expectation or result as an outcome is a bad question. That doesn't mean that scientific discoveries have not been made this way, because they have, but for your science fair project it is important to stick to the standard acceptable process.

o   If I eat a chemically grown apple, what happens?
o   Does music affect plants?
o   Are people born under the sign Libra more indecisive?
o   Which tastes better, Diet Coke or Regular Coke? (subjective responses)
o   Do snakes make good pets?
o   How do you grow an apple?

Science Fair Project Big Question Outcomes Checklist

Print this page, truthfully check off all the criteria for writing a good question, and attach the form to your Science Log. Date your entry.

I have an excellent Big Question because....	✓
I have written the specific question that I am most curious about.	
I have chosen my topic.	
I can design a "fair test" to answer my Big Question.	
I can change only one variable at a time and control the other factors (variables) that might influence my experiment so that they do not interfere with each other.	
My experiment is safe to do. It meets the safety standards outlined by Intel ISEP and my school's rules.	
I have enough time to perform 3 trials of my experiment.	
My experiment meets all the school's science fair rules.	
Check one choice: o My science fair project requires SRC (Scientific Review Committee) approval. o My science fair project does not require SRC (Scientific Review Committee) approval.	
I read the List of Science Fair Projects to Avoid and I avoided them.	

You have accomplished a gigantic step today. Now you have found your perfect, "just right" topic. Congratulations!!! You laid the foundation.

Proposal Form
Letter "U" on the Timeline

Take out the printed Proposal Form. Fill it out. Make 2 copies, one for your teacher and one for your parents. Place your copy in the Science Log.

Why do you need a Proposal Form for your science fair project?
Contracts are a part of life. They spell out terms and conditions so that everyone's responsibilities and expectations are met.

A science fair project Proposal Form is a contract you make mostly with yourself. You and one of your parents both sign and date it before turning it in to your teacher. It is important to hand in your proposal before you get started on your experiment. Your teacher may ask you to make some changes or s/he may not approve your proposal at all. Better to get it approved before starting your experiment.

2nd Meeting with Your Teacher & Parent(s)
Getting the Go Ahead
Letter "T" on the Timeline

Meet with your teacher within the next couple of days. Bring your Science Log and Proposal Form. These two items will show her how serious you are about your project and all the thought and work you already put into it.

Remember the secret to enrolling (influencing) someone? Radiate your smile from within! Share your enthusiasm about your science topic. Be a good listener.

Take out your Science Log and show her your category of science, subcategory of science and Big Question.

Once your project is approved, meet with one or both of your parents. (Remember that enthusiastic attitude.)

In your Science Log, input the date and what transpired at the meeting with your teacher.

Meeting with your Parent(s)
Sit down with one or both of your parents, show them your Science Log and inform them of your topic. Tell them that you met with your teacher and have her approval to move ahead with your project. Together, set a realistic budget. Remember to show your enthusiasm! And listen carefully to what they have to say.

How much money will you spend? Well, that depends on your family's household budget. A science fair project can be simple and inexpensive. Do not make it so complicated that you will not want to finish it.

Make a shopping list of what supplies you will need.

Input into your Science Log the date and what you discussed with your parent(s). Tape or staple this Form into your Science Log. Date the entry.

II - Background Research

Purpose of Background Research

Have you ever heard the expression "re-inventing the wheel"? You definitely don't want to do that, but how do you avoid needlessly starting from scratch? By taking advantage of the knowledge and experience of others. That's where background research comes in.

It pays to first do your research before going to the library, talking with experts, looking on the internet before designing your experiment. The plan will give you a reliable roadmap to help you find your way from questions to answers without taking unnecessary detours.

You will need at least 3 resources as references. Intel ISEF requires "5 major references – science journal articles, books, Internet sites." Some teachers require original research. (Will discuss this later in the chapter).

Benefits of Doing Background Research

Once you have decided what experiment you want to tackle, you need to do background research on your topic. It is important to find out what research and experiments have been done and what they found out.

1. Gives you a broad overview of the subject.

2. You will come across definitions of the topic.

3. Will give you an introduction to key issues.

4. Gives identifying important facts related to your project – terminology, dates, events, history, names of experts in the field, and professional organizations.

5. Helps to find more keywords and subject-specific vocabulary terms that can be used for database searches.

6. Get suggestions about where to find resources and materials that assist you better in understanding your project. The more specific questions you ask, the more helpful the responses will be.

7. Helps to refine your topic. If you are finding too much information, your topic may be too broad. The research will help you find more specific information you may want to focus on.

8. Determine what predictions you can make about your experiment based on what you understand of the theory behind it. Regardless of whether your prediction turns out right or wrong, you will have come to understand the causes of what happened or why something failed to happen. And that is exactly what science fair judges are looking for.

9. Find out what techniques and equipment others have used for investigating the topic.

10. Discover what mistakes others have made.

11. Leads you to more interesting questions to ask about your experiment.

12. Find mathematical equations that will help to explain aspects of your project,

13. Leads to bibliographies that can be used to find additional sources of information about your experiment.

14. Expands upon the key points stated in the introduction of your project paper.

15. Helps your reader determine if you have a basic understanding of the research problem being investigated and promotes confidence in the overall quality of your analysis and findings. This information provides the reader with the essential context needed to understand the research problem and its significance.

Three Types of Background Research that Engineers Use

1. **Observation** – observe users in the environment where the problem exists or while a similar product is being used.

2. **Examination and Analysis** – examine and analyze similar products and solutions. Ask if you can take them apart. You will learn from other's experiences.

3. **Library and Internet Research** – Find other products similar to what you want to create or improve upon.

Creating a Background Research Plan
Overview
Before you actually do your research, you will need to have a few tools in place:
I.   Learn about the different types of scientific investigations.

II.   Learn how to create a Bibliography, which includes how to take notes and organize the information you gather.

44

III. Learn the kinds of questions to ask to find the information you will need before doing your research, writing your hypothesis and designing your experiment.

Details

I. Different Types of Scientific Investigations

 #6:

Before you begin your background research, it is important to know the various types of investigation.

INVESTIGATIVE - This is a project that asks a question, constructs a hypothesis, draws a conclusion and then tests that hypothesis by constructing an experiment using the scientific method.

LABORATORY DEMONSTRATION - This is a project that repeats an "experiment" found in science activity books, textbooks, workbooks and encyclopedias. No unique questions are explored.

REPORT AND POSTER - This is a project based on extensive research done in books and other materials in order to write a paper on the chosen topic. Posters (display boards) are then used to illustrate key concepts from the research paper.

HOBBY or SHOW-AND-TELL - This is a project that consists of either a collection of objects or features interesting artifacts. Involves library research but no hypothesis is tested.

MODEL BUILDING - This is a project which involves the construction of a model that may illustrate a scientific principle.

ENGINEERING DESIGN PROCESS - Design and construct an engineered product for target users to do some useful function. Examples: robot, device, program for a computer. You are not allowed to use a kit. The project must be original.

Most regional and state fairs require the Investigative or the Engineering Design Process type of project. This book only discusses the Scientific Method.

II. Explains what information you will need to gather in order to write your Bibliography and what kind of system you need to have in place to keep this information organized.

Bibliography
Letter "R" on the Timeline

Overview
IMPORTANT: You are not ready to actually do research or write a bibliography. First you need more information: what a bibliography is and what it includes, how to take notes, how to format a bibliography, how to find original research, and interview experts. Hang in there and read the next several pages.

The Bibliography is a carefully organized, written list of references for each source that you cite in your Project Report. This list, written in a specific way, is called a **Bibliography**. These are required standards for research papers to follow when you document your sources. All of them contain the author's name; title of the book, magazine or journal; the date the material was published; and the source - who published the information.

Before you develop a background research plan for your science fair project, you will need to have a system in place to put all the information you gather from references, text books, newspapers, journals, magazine articles, websites, interviews, and wherever else your search takes you.

Keep track of each source as you find it.

The following gives general information on a variety of topics. These are considered to be **general reference sources**, meaning that they provide facts and knowledge that can be used as a foundation for your research. You only need to spend a little time using these resources but they will save you a tremendous amount of time when searching in databases and more subject-specific resources: almanacs, bibliographies, biographical resources, dictionaries, directories, encyclopedias, handbooks, statistical sources, thesauruses.

Use **primary sources** such as original research (will go into detail later in this chapter), talking with experts, interviewing target users and customers, and from your own experience.

Then research **secondary sources** such magazines, books, articles, textbooks or Internet sites.

There are two ways to record and keep track of your references: 1) a bibliography worksheet and 2) index cards.

I know you are getting anxious to get started, but don't. Keep on reading. I will tell you when to begin your research.

Bibliography Worksheet
- o Use the 4 sheets you printed of the **Bibliography Worksheet**. You may not need to use all the sheets or you may need more.

- o Keep a list of all the books, articles, websites and interviews as you gather information for your science fair project in your Science Log or on notecards.

- o You will need **three to five written sources at a minimum** to create the bibliography, which will become part of your final report.

- o For each website write the following information:
  - The author's full name, if it is listed
  - The page title
  - The name of the company that posted the page
  - The web address (URL) for the page
  - The date you last looked at the page
    You'll find most of this information in a website's "about" or "contact" page, or at the page's header or footer.

- o Cut the sections of the Bibliography Worksheet that you used and tape or staple it into your Science Log when complete. Date the entry.

Bibliography Formats
There are various types of bibliography formats. U.S. schools usually ask their students to use the MLA (Modern Language Association) and the APA (American Psychological Association).

- o MLA - English and humanities instructors ask you to document your sources with the MLA system of citations. The MLA calls the bibliography, *Works Cited*. https://tinyurl.com/y87kr2du

- o APA - Many social science instructors ask you to document your sources with the APA system of in-text citations and references. The APA use the term, *The Reference List*. https://tinyurl.com/y7tk3zt9

- o CSE (Council of Science Editors) is used by many science teachers. https://tinyurl.com/yapb4ccm

Some people use a mixture of all three types of listings:
- o APA to format for online sources
- o MLA to format all other sources
- o CSE to format citations from articles

Ask your teacher which format to follow if s/he did not tell you what to do.
Dixie State University Library shows you how to format each type of bibliography style.
https://tinyurl.com/yaoc9vnj

How to Write Note Cards

You are going to need a system to organize the information you find when doing your research. Having a system of taking notes will make it easier to do this. A recommended method is to use note cards / index cards.

An easy way of collecting your references and keeping them in order is to use 4" x 6" or 3" x 5" note cards. To keep them organized, use a rubber band to secure them. When you are ready to formulate your Bibliography, it is easy to put them in alphabetical order. Keep them in a safe place.

You are going to have two different kinds of cards: 1) source cards 2) information cards.

Source Note Cards

Use the **white cards** to track where you found each piece of information. Number the cards for each source. If you need more than one card per source then number them this way: Source 1-A, Source 1-B.

o   In the upper left corner write the keyword phrase or subject.

o   In the upper right corner write the number of the source.

science fair projects	No. 1

Binder, Madeline, M.S. Ed, M.S. Human Services Counseling
2022
Student's Guide to Science Fair Projects, Step-by-Step for a
Winning Edge
Evanston, IL
M-ZAN Solutions, Inc (publisher)
(eBook)

The following is the information you will need to write on your bibliography source cards:

o   **Interviews**
Last name of person interviewed. First name. Type of reference: Interview. Interviewer's Name. Date of interview.

o   **Books**
Title of book, author name (last name first), publisher, copyright date, city and state where published, pages read or quoted

o   **Journals and Science Magazines**
Name, volume, number, date of publication, title of article, author and pages read or quoted

- **Newspapers**
  Name, date, section and pages of newspaper, author, title of article

- **Encyclopedia**
  Name, volume, number, publisher, copyright date, title, author, pages of article

- **Science Fair Software Packages**
  Name of program, version or release number, name of supplier, and place where supplier is located

- **Documents online**
  Title, author and date of article, organization that posted the document, organization's location and online address.

List all the sources alphabetically. In cases where you don't have an author's name, write the title and insert it into the list, keeping the alphabetical order.

Information Note Cards

The 2nd set of cards is called information note cards. They will be used to collect the information that answers your keyword questions (explained in detail later on in this book). The information gathered will be used to refine your experiment procedure and write your Research Report. If you prefer to type notes directly into an electronic device, be sure to keep track of your sources.

Always keep in mind the purpose of your research paper: it is to give you information so you have an understanding as to the results of your experiment.

- List the key points and quotes, and put the name of the source at the top of the card. Each card will be from one source that answers a keyword question. You may have more than one source per question.

- Use a different color notecard for each keyword phrase.

- The following template will show you what information you need to write on the notecard and where to place the information. (see example on next page)

Keyword / Keyword Phrase	Source #
Keyword Question	
Quote or notes you put into your own word from the reference.	
	Author's Last Name / Page(s)

- In the upper right corner of each card write the Number of the card. This number will correspond to the number of the source on the Bibliography Worksheet printable or notecard that you use to document your references.

- Number the cards for each source. If you need to use more than one card per source: Example – Source 1-A, Source 1-B

- In the upper left corner of the card write the keyword phrase or subject.

- In the lower right corner write the author's last name and the pages where you found the information.

- Write a single thought on each card that paraphrases the text. If you want to write a direct quote, make sure that you place parentheses around the quote so that you give proper credit in your paper.

free wind blade turbine	#1
Who invented the free wind blade turbine?	

Chris Gabrys and Tim Rodgers, and Mike Hess, a successful entrepreneur and former CEO, Windspire Energy

This came from an email response 9/5/16

Email from owner of Windspire: Richard Kline

Note Taking Tips

- **Paraphrasing vs. Plagiarism**
  Paraphrasing is writing something in your own words. It means that you completely restate the complete thought. Replacing a couple of words is not good enough; you need to make what you write your own.

  Plagiarism is copying another person's words as if they were your own. This is true whether the source is a book, journal, reference book or from the Internet. This is like stealing something from someone else. So be sure to put quotes around something that you copy.

- **What to include in your research paper**
  - History of similar experiments or inventions

  - Definition of all important words, terminology and concepts relevant to your experiment

- Answers to all your background research questions

- Mathematical formulas (if any) in order to show the results of your experiment

o **Quoting Text**

If you using the author's own words, phrase, sentence or paragraph, you must put them in quotation marks. When interviewing someone, ask if you can quote them.

Example:
"All life is an experiment. The more experiments you make the better."
(Emerson – 1860)

o **Citations**

In writing your research paper, it's okay to copy pictures, diagrams or ideas from one of your sources – as long as you give credit to the author or source. You do this with a citation using the author's name and publication date (Jones, 2010) at the end of the sentence but before the period.

Document all facts, pictures, diagrams, illustrations, charts and graphs. Write the author's name and date of each publication immediately following the reference.

Summary: Background research tells you...
o What has been done to prove a similar hypothesis?
o What knowledge and science limitations will limit your experiment?
o What previous experiments may be improved upon?

In other words, find out what others already know and did!

You are now ready to do your Background Research.

You are going to develop a knowledge base of information before you design your experiment. You will be conducting a variety of information searches and compiling all the information in a useful way.

III.Create Your Background Research Plan by finding keywords, using the question keyword worksheet, networking, and talking with experts. This information will help you to develop a thorough knowledge base related to your experiment. You do this by conducting a variety of information searches and compiling all the information in a useful way.

First use primary sources such as talking with local experts or from your own experiences. Then research secondary sources such as encyclopedias, subject-related encyclopedias, dictionaries, magazines, books, articles bases, textbooks or Internet sites. At least 3 to 5 research sources must be used. Check with your teacher to see how many you need.

Determine the Keywords
Letter "R" on the Timeline

Use the **Keyword Worksheet** printable that you printed for this section. Follow the instructions on the sheet as you read the information and directions below.

No. 1 – Determine Your Keywords
Research the Who, What, Where, Why, When and How

You'll find the keywords for you experiment in your project question, but also brainstorm for additional keywords and other concepts you want to explore.

When you search for your keyword phrase, look at the bottom of the search engines' pages. You will see more suggested keyword phrases. You can also delete some words from each keyword phrase to simplify your search.

Bing Keyword Toolbox (https://tinyurl.com/yymroroj) and Google Keyword Toolbox (https://keywordtool.io/) are free keyword search engines. Before you register, if you are under the age of 18, check with your parents to see if it is OK to sign up.

No. 2 – Write Questions Pertaining to the Keywords
The following information gives you a plan of action. The **Keyword Question Worksheet** is an excellent way to generate ideas for your background research.
Use the **Keyword Question Worksheet** that you printed. It will help you to develop keyword questions. You will need to identify questions to find what other experiments have been done.

The secret to using the worksheet is to write questions for each of your keywords and then decide the ones that are relevant to your topic. Fill in the blanks for each question pertaining to your subject.

o You will be using what, when, where, how, does, why, and which to help you transform your keywords into more specific research questions. Come up with as many keywords and questions as you can, then go back later to eliminate any that are not relevant to your project.

Example of Questions:
What is the difference between horizontal and vertical wind turbines?
When are hydro wind turbines used?
Where is it best to grow mold in your house?
How does a solar panel work?

Does sun energy produce more power than wind energy?
Why do caterpillars turn into butterflies?

The questions are examples to help you get started with your keyword search. Develop own questions related to your project.

o   You may find a lot of interesting questions to research, but they do not have anything to do with your experiment. These are called irrelevant questions. Later you will have to eliminate those questions that do not really have much to do with your experiment and would, therefore, not be helpful to answer.

   Be aware that a question might seem irrelevant on the surface but may be worth exploring at some future point. In that case, set it aside and come back to it later when you can look at it with fresh eyes.

   For example, it might be interesting to know about the history of wind turbines, but not necessarily important to your research project if you are researching the efficiency of vertical wind turbine blades.

   If you are not sure whether or not a question is relevant then ask the opinion of others who may know more about your subject, such as parents, teachers and mentors. If you cannot find out about the relevancy of a question, don't worry about it. The answer will come apparent when you do your experiment.

o   Be fearless. Ask advice from your parents, teachers and experts in your field of interest. Their experiences could help you to define your project, clearly refine your experiments, and give you a wider perspective on what you are want to accomplish.

Example of a Keyword Question Chart
When I did a search for *quiet wind turbine experimental kit* or *propeller free vertical wind turbine experiment kit*, nothing came up. Then I used the term, *wind turbine experiment kit* and *propeller free turbine*.

Organic vs. Certified Organic Food

Questions	Keywords to Search	Possible Questions to do Background Research	Is the Question Relevant
Who	certified organic food	Who needs to know the difference between organic and certified organic food? Who discovered organic / certified organic food?	Yes, for health reasons, some people need to know this info No
What		What is the difference between organic and certified organic food? What properties are contained in certified organic food that are absent from organic food? (or vice versa) What soil conditions must exist for a food to be considered organic and certified organic?	Yes, for all questions
When		When does a person know whether or not a food is organic or certified organic? When did people become interested in certified organic food?	Yes No
Where		Where is organic food grown? Where is certified organic food grown?	No
Why		Why is there organic food? Why is there certified organic food?	No Yes
How		How is certified organic food labeled?	Yes, consumers need to be educated and made aware of differences.

After you have completed using the Question Keyword Word Worksheet, tape or staple it into your Science Log. Remember to date the entry and any brief notes you need to add.

Keyword & Question Checklist

Print the checklist. Check all the tasks that you completed. Don't move on to the next page until you complete all the tasks. Attach the checklist to your Science Log and date the entry.

Check off all the outcomes you accomplished.	✓
I have identified all the keywords related to my project and completed the worksheet.	
○ I have completed the Keyword Question Worksheet for each of my keywords. ○ I have removed irrelevant questions, but put them aside in case I need them later. ○ The answers to my research questions gave me the information I need to do my experiment. ○ One or more of my research questions specifically asks about the equipment or techniques I may need to do my experiment.	

After you have completed this section, pat yourself on the back for a job well done.

Tips for Finding Reputable Research

The Judges will check to see if you used original research. Original research is the report of a study written by the researchers who actually did the study. The researchers describe their hypothesis or BIG question and the purpose of the study. The researchers detail their research methods.

Remember, your number one goal is to find original research. Don't get discouraged if this takes time. Follow the instructions below and you will find what you are looking for. It is important to stay focused on one task at a time, otherwise it can become overwhelming. Use your Science Log to stay organized.

○ One way to stay on task when you are doing research is to use your Keyword Question Worksheet plus the few questions you wrote after meeting with experts. Then research the answers to those questions.

○ If you live near a university, their library will have professional journals. They also will have copies of their graduate students' theses.

○ It is very important to primarily use scientific literature as references opposed to popular literature such as magazines and newspapers.

o Your library science teacher is a key person to help you find information. Like a great sleuth, uncover as much as possible about your topic before conducting your experiment. This helps you to understand your topic.

o Look at the date on the research pertaining to your topic. Science information gets outdated fast.

o During the time you are doing your research, keep a page in your Science Log that is titled: *Possible Supplies I Will Need for My Project.*

Library Research – the most valuable resource at a local library or college library is the librarian. Make friends with the librarian. In fact, make her your best friend. S/he will become an integral part of your networking team. If you live near a college or university, visit their library. It has professional journals, magazines, and copies of their graduate students' theses.

From the librarian you can learn how to organize your research, search for information, read and use citations, narrow down web searches, and weed out the excellent and poor resources.

Some libraries have vertical reference services where you can chat online, email or talk on the phone to a reference librarian.

o First get an overview of what your subject is about. General information can be found in a dictionary, encyclopedia or textbook for each of your keywords. There are also specialized dictionaries and encyclopedias such as science, music, sports, etc.

o At your local library or college library you will find periodicals (magazines and newspapers). Look to see which articles have resources listed at the end of the article. Bibliographies at the back of an article or books list sources that can lead you to original research and experts.

o Many school or local libraries pay a fee to use online resources that are not accessible to the public or are too expensive for individuals to join. You can use the program in the library or sometimes login with your library card number. "ERIC" is an excellent program to use to find original research. See how Eric search works (https://eric.ed.gov/)

o Most libraries, whether they are small or large, are part of an interlibrary loan program where they loan books and periodicals for a specific period of time. Sometimes there is a small fee per book ($1.00).

o Most books have a table of contents and an Appendix. Check these sections to see if a book has the information you need.

Internet Research – The Internet can be a valuable resource, but you need be careful of where the information originates. Textbooks and other publications typically go through a rigorous fact-checking process, but for much Internet material, there is usually no comparable effort.

- o **Internet Safety Tips <u>Before</u> Doing Your Research**: Discuss this section with your parent(s).

   Do not use your home address, telephone number, usernames, screen names, birthday, school name, your name or any personal information that could identify you in your email address.

   Nothing is private on the Internet, not even blogs! So don't reveal any personal information about yourself. And don't put your photo in a blog or online.

   Never engage in an online communication with a stranger, even if s/he says they know your parents, teacher or friend of a friend.

- o Search engines are excellent ways to search by keywords on the Internet. They try to index everything.
  Google (https://www.google.com/)
  JISC (https://tinyurl.com/yckujh69),
  Rasmussen.edu (https://tinyurl.com/4crzf4z5)
  Yahoo (https://www.yahoo.com/)
  Refseek (https://www.refseek.com/) Academic search engine for students and scholars).

- o Subject Portals are more selective than search engines and list a small part of the information. The sites have been checked for relevance unlike the search engines. Here are the most popular:
  Librarians' Index to the Internet (https://lili.org/)
  The WWW Virtual Library (http://vlib.org/)

- o Organizations and societies have online databases. If you call them, they may help with up-to-date resources.

- o Take accurate notes on your note cards. List all the references, where you found them, name of reference, author, date, etc.

Continued on next page

○ Evaluate each source and decide if it is an excellent or a poor source:

Excellent References	Poor References
Comes from a credible source. The information makes sense.	Comes from a source with poor credibility.
The researcher is an expert in his/her field.	Person researching or writing the reference is not an expert in the field.
Researcher does not have vested interest in the outcome of the test results.	The researcher works for the company/subsidiary of the company that manufacturers the item.
Has up-to-date information.	Has out of date information.
Is not biased – doesn't take a point of view.	Is not objective and fair – takes one point of view.
Does not have errors when compared to other resources.	Have errors when compared to other resources.
Cites the original source in a proper way.	Does not cite where the information came from. Has no index or resources.
The reference material is easy to find.	The reference material is difficult to find.

Tips on Using Search Engines - Often times your search brings up too much information or too many irrelevant sources. Here are some tips on how to narrow your search and get specific information about your subject matter:

○ **Do a very specific keyword phrase search**. For instance, if you are doing an experiment about wind turbines, this is too general of a search term. How about … **most efficient shape of wind turbine blades**. If you get too many extraneous sources, then put your keyword phrase in parentheses: **"most efficient shape for wind turbine blades"**.

○ Sites that give you search tips:
Berkley.edu (https://tinyurl.com/leqf)
Google Support (https://tinyurl.com/qx88vdg)

Networking is an important process to learn when doing research.

○ **Ask questions of people from various backgrounds and specialties** to assist with researching what experiments have been done in your field of interest. Ask your teacher, mentor, parents, students who have completed science fair projects that used the scientific method.

○ **Interview experts in your field of interest**. They have a wealth of information they can impart to you.

Write a Letter of Inquiry

Your complete name
Your street address
Your city, state, zip code

Person's First and Last name you are writing to
Name of company (if you are sending the letter to his/her place of work)
Street address
City, State, Zip Code

Month, Day, Year

Dear (Dr., Mr., Mrs., Ms or Sir):
I am a student at Jones School in the (grade level) and am doing my science fair project on quiet wind turbines. I understand that you are a wind turbine expert.

I would appreciate you answering one or all of the following questions and sending any relevant information that you may have as soon as possible.

(insert your questions here)

Thank you very much for your time and effort,

 (sign your name here)

(Print by hand or input on the computer your name here.)

Show the letter to one of your parents and ask permission to include your telephone number and email address.

Sometimes it helps to enclose a self-addressed, stamped envelope.

If you can contact the person via email, you may receive the information sooner and it is much less expensive than snail mail.

o   **How to Interview Experts**
     The experience of others is part of a background research plan and also part of not "reinventing the wheel". Network to find people you want to interview who are considered experts in their field, people who have taken some classes on the subject, or have completed a science fair project similar to yours: professors, doctors, lawyers, veterinarians, researchers, science teacher, friends' parents, and authors of the articles you read. Local research firms will have experts who may also help. You may interview the expert in person, on the phone, or over the Internet.

Don't be intimidated when it comes to networking. Everyone does it. You have even experienced networking when you were deciding what kind of cell phone you wanted. You probably talked with various friends and family members to find out what phone they enjoyed using the most. Become an expert networker and you will create a unique and excellent science fair project.

PLEASE do not, I repeat... DO NOT ask anyone for a science fair project. Experts are strictly there to help with giving you information in their field of expertise.

How to Schedule a Meeting with an Expert

Make an appointment with an expert, either by phone, email, or text. Agree to the amount of time to talk. Ask the expert the best way to conduct the interview: Google Meet, Zoom, Skype, Facetime or telephone.

A good rule is to limit the interview to 20 minutes. Ask permission to record the interview. Wear a watch or have some kind of time piece in front of you.
- Start on time and stop on time.

- If you want to record the interview, ask the expert if it OK to do so.

- Use the User Interview Worksheet or Question Worksheet for each interview. This will keep your answers organized.

- Sincerely thank the person for his / her time and information.

- After the interview, listen to the recording. Write in your Science Log the person's name, company, position, expertise, date of interview. Either write a thank you note and mail it the next day or send one via email. Free online thank you eCards can be found on Paperless (https://www.paperlesspost.com/).

- **Ask very specific questions**. Solid questions tend to yield good, solid answers that will help move your project to a successful conclusion. Be quick, efficient and smooth. In other words, be prepared.

Sample Questions to Ask an Expert

Choose your questions from your **Question Worksheet**. Use it as a guide. Write your questions in advance and bring them with you to the meeting. You only have 10 to 20 minutes, so choose the questions that are most relevant to your project research.

Here are 6 examples:
1. What science concepts are best to study to better understand my project?

2. What role do the shape and size of the wind turbine blades play in its energy efficiency?
3. What physical forces are involved in having a wind turbine work efficiently?

4. How does a wind turbine with blades differ from a WindSpire vertical wind turbine in terms of efficiency?

5. Do KN95 masks really protect a person from getting viruses?

6. How many times can a person wear a mask before the fibers get overloaded with germs and no longer protect us?

Tips
o   Know what you are going to ask before you do.

o   Give a gentle elbow bump if you meet in person. Thank the expert for meeting with you.

o   Ask if they can lead you to resources or more experts.

o   When you are finished, ask if you can quote them as a source in your report. Then, on a note card, write their information.

o   Give an elbow bump again when the meeting is over.

o   Hand write, email text or snail mail a thank you to the person for contributing their time and expertise.

How to Find an Expert on the Internet
Do a search in Google, Bing or Firefox. Search for the keyword phrase, *ask a _____ expert*.

Examples: *ask a physics expert* or *ask a wind turbine expert*.

Just Answer (https://www.justanswer.com/) has experts from various fields:

What is Original Research?

Judges will check to see if you used original research. Research that comes from a primary source is considered original research. An article is considered original research if the...

- report of a study is written by the researchers who actually did the study.

- researchers describe their hypothesis or research question and the purpose of the study.

- researchers detail their research methods.

- results of the research are reported.

- researchers interpret their results and discuss possible implications.

How Do You Know if the Article is Original Research?

There is no one way to easily tell if an article is a research article like there is for peer-reviewed articles in the Ulrich's database. The only way to be sure is to read the article to verify that it is written by the researchers and that they have explained all of their findings, in addition to listing their methodologies, results, and any conclusions based on the evidence collected.

However, there are a few key indicators that will help you to quickly decide whether or not your article is based on original research.

- View the PDF version so you can plainly see the major subdivisions that need to be present in a research article:
    - Literature Review or Background
    - Methods
    - Results
    - Conclusions
    - Discussion

- Read through the abstract (summary) before you attempt to find the full-text PDF. The abstract of the article usually contains those subdivision headings where the key sections are summarized individually.

- Ask your librarian to see if she has access to scholarly journals and research databases.

Where to Find Original Research
Overview

- The easiest way to begin is by looking up each of your keywords in an encyclopedia or textbook. This will give you general information and help orient you to your subject. Text books and encyclopedias include bibliographies that can be used as sources that can lead you to other sources.

- Specialty magazines target a specific interest report on research projects. Listed at the end of the articles are the sources of the original research.
Professional journals and trade publications can also be good sources of information. Your library has an Index of magazines and journals, as well as a directory of professional associations. Most associations have their own publications, with information that may not yet have appeared in textbooks.

Bibliography Outcomes Checklist

Print each checklist below. After you checked each, attach the checklist to your Science Log and date the entry. Then move on to the next checklist.

I have completed by Bibliography because...	✓
I have 3 to 5 primary references on my science fair topic.	
All my references include the information required by APA, MLA or CSE writing style.	
All my references include required information: author's name, title of the book or article, date and place of publication.	
All my references are listed in alphabetical order, starting with last name, then first name. (You will need to do this when you type your Project Report.)	
I have at least one reference for each of my research questions.	
I taped / stapled the Background Project Research Worksheet in the Science Log and dated the entry.	
I taped / stapled the Big Question Worksheet in the Science Log and dated the entry.	
I taped / stapled the Bibliography Worksheet in the Science Log and dated the entry.	

Background Research Outcomes Checklist

Check off all the outcomes you accomplished.	✓
I have identified all the keywords for my science fair project question.	
I have used the question word table to generate research questions.	
I have thrown out irrelevant questions.	
The answers to my research questions gave me the information I need to design an experiment and predict the outcome.	
One or more of my research questions specifically asks about equipment or techniques I will need to perform an experiment (if applicable).	
I networked and asked specific questions related to my project. Interviewed friends, family, teachers and experts. Sent them thank you notes.	

Now that you checked off all the tasks in both the above checklists, you can move on to the next section of this book. Have fun!

III - How to Construct a Hypothesis

 #7

What is the Difference Between Fact, Theory and Hypothesis?

A fact is something that has actual existence. At the very least it is a piece of information that is presented as provable. Facts are true, provable, observable, measurable, recorded, confirmed, and indisputable. The clues or signal words are numbers, statistics, documents, eye-witnesses (many times reliability is questionable), video footage, photograph, or / and recordings.

For example: Two of my neighbors reported to the police that they saw a bear knock down three garbage cans in our neighborhood.

Sometimes facts are disproved. Up until the year 1992 Pluto was considered to be the 9th planet from the sun. Now it is called a dwarf planet. So, are facts really facts?

Theory

A theory is a logical explanation or model based on observations, facts, hypotheses, experimentation, and reasoning that attempts to explain a range of natural phenomena. Theories are constantly subject to testing, modification, and refutation as new evidence and ideas emerge. Theories also have predictive capabilities that guide further investigation.

Hypothesis

"A scientific hypothesis that survives experimental testing becomes a scientific theory." (showmeword.com) A hypothesis is an educational guess or prediction of what you think will happen.

Variables
Letter "Q" on the Timeline

All scientists, students or professionals do experiments to search for cause-and-effect relationships in nature or products. They want to find out what changes occur when one item causes something else to vary in a predictable way.

These changing quantities are called **variables**. A variable is any factor, trait or condition that can exist in differing amounts or types. Variables are the things that have an effect on the experiment such as amount of light, temperature, humidity, time changes, or plant growth.

There are 3 kinds of variables that are present in most experiments: independent, dependent, and controlled.

○ **Independent Variable** (I.V.) – the factor that either changes on its own or the scientist purposely changes it. To insure a fair test an experiment has only one independent variable. As the independent variable changes, the scientist observes what happens.

The goal of an experimental investigation is to determine how changes in an independent variable affects another variable, which is called the dependent variable.

○ **Dependent Variable** (D.V.) – scientists focus his / her observations to see how it responds to the change made to the independent variable. The new value of the dependent variable is caused by and depends on the value of the independent variable. There may be more than one dependent variable.

○ **Controlled Variables** / Constant Variables (C.V.) – quantities that the scientist wants to remain constant. S/he observes them as closely as the dependent variables. Most experiments have more than one controlled variable.

Example I: Object as a Variable
- **Controlled variables**: Take a package of sunflower seeds. Use two containers that are the same size with the same kind of potting soil. Have them exposed to the same amount of light and air. Plant half the package of seeds in one pot. Space them equal distance as you did with the seeds in the other container. Water the plants with equal amounts of water.

- **Independent Variable**: Feed one set of seeds with fertilizer.

- **Dependent Variable**: Do not feed the seeds in the second container. Which seeds germinate the fastest?

Example II: Time as an I.V.
Over time the dependent variable changes. You start the process and then observe and record data at regular intervals.

Example III: I.V. for **Surveys and Tests of Different Groups**
In order for a survey to have validity, you will need to have a large number of participants in each group that you survey.

SurveyMonkey gives an excellent explanation of a good estimate of the margin of error (confidence interval). If you are going to do a survey, it is imperative that you read this. https://tinyurl.com/2fy7s2ez

The people of the survey or groups define the I.V. For example,
The Big Question: Who listens to classical music the most, teenagers or their parents?
- I.V. : Groups receiving the survey: teenagers and parents.

- D. V. : Amount of time each person listens to classical music per day measured in hours.

- C. V. : Ask the question in exactly the same way to each individual

Example IV: Either/Or (Binary) Variables
Something might be either present or not present during an experiment.

Big Question: Is a classroom noisier when there is a substitute teacher?
- I.V. : Teacher location: either the substitute teacher or the regular teacher is in the classroom. The teacher's location is an either/or situation.

- D. V. : Loudness measured in decibels

- C.V. : Same classroom, same students, same time of day

Simple Explanation of Variables

Doing a Fair Test
A fair test means that you change one factor (variable) while keeping all the other conditions the same.

Conducting a fair test is one of the most important aspects of doing a science fair project. To do a fair test you must only change one factor at a time while keeping all other conditions the same. The changing factors in an experiment are called variables.

For example, let's say that you want to measure which wind turbine produces the most electrical energy as measured by a multimeter, a vertical axis turbine or a horizontal axis turbine. Would it be a fair test if you gave the first wind turbine a gentle start and allowed the 2nd wind turbine to start on its own? The only variable that must change is the turbine, and they both need to start exactly at the same time and in the same way, with no interference by the tester.

Here is another example… suppose you do an experiment to see if fertilizer makes a plant grow to be larger than a plant that is not fed fertilizer. You have six different pots; use the same amount of sand in each of the 6 pots. Add the same amount of fertilizer to 3 of the pots. Put the same number of seeds in each pot, at the same depth, and the same distance apart from each other. Put all the pots in the same location and water each one with the same amount of water every day. Which of the pots produced the largest plants? Is that a fair test? Yes.

An unfair test would be if you put rich soil and fertilizer in 3 of the pots and 3 of the pots had sand, because then you would be changing 2 factors.

Measuring Variables: A science fair project requires you to express results in some measurable way. Decide on what the variables will be and how you will measure them.

Use a specific numerical measurement of quantity such as length, weight, velocity, time, voltage, and so forth.
You could also consider using a variable with no quantity, for example, an absence of light (vs. presence of light).

Make sure you will have enough time to complete the experiment. It's a good idea to do a practice run to work out any problems you might encounter.

Advanced Topics

Some experiments do not show that a change in the independent variable will cause a change in the dependent variable. Instead, the independent variable may only be related to the dependent variable. This relationship is called a correlation.

For instance, do calluses on a man's hands have anything to do with their profession? You may notice that men with calluses on their hands are carpenters. Does that mean that all men who have calluses on their hands are carpenters?

What if a lawyer is an avid canoeist on weekends or just returned from a 2-week vacation where he canoed every day for 6 hours a day? Would he have calluses on his hands if he didn't wear gloves?

Write Your Variables

Now it is your turn to decide your variables. Establish the variables important to your experiment.

Take out your printed Variables Worksheet. Write your variables in the worksheet.

After you have completed writing you variables, move on to the next page to complete the Outcomes Checklist.

Variable(s) Outcomes Checklist

Print the checklist. Check off all the tasks that you have completed. Once all the entries have been checked, attach the checklist to your Science Log and date the entry.

My Variables are excellent because....	✓
My independent variable is measurable.	
I changed the independent variable during the experiment.	
I identified all relevant dependent variables.	
My dependent variables are caused by and dependent on the independent variable.	
All my dependent variable(s) are measurable.	
I have identified all relevant controlled variables.	
All controlled variables can be held at a steady value during the experiment.	

Writing Your Hypothesis

Key Information
○ Now you are going to turn your Big Question into a statement.

○ The most important part of doing your science fair project is designing and writing your hypothesis because your entire experiment is based on your research. It is the foundation of your whole project.

○ When you build a house, if your foundation is not strong, then the house will fall down. The same is true of your hypothesis.

A hypothesis is an educated guess or prediction of what you think will happen. What makes this section so much fun is that there is no right or wrong answer. It is what you <u>think</u> is the answer to the Big Question.

A good hypothesis takes the form of
"If I do this _____, then _____ will happen."

For example, I hypothesize that flower seeds fed an organic natural fertilizer will germinate faster than those that are fed a synthetic chemical fertilizer.

○ Even if your experiment produces different results from your hypothesis statement, do not change your statement.

3 Step Process to Writing a Testable Hypothesis
Think of a general hypothesis. This includes everything you have observed and reviewed when you gathered information during your Project Research. This stage is often called the **Research Problem**.

1. **Examples of How to Write a Hypothesis**
   A student notices that when he eats a vegetable or a fruit that is not organic, he gets shaky. He wants to find out why. His research leads him to believe that chemically grown food can cause some people's pulse to race (become rapid). The student proposes a general hypothesis. *"Synthetic chemical fertilizers when used in growing vegetables or fruits affect a person."*

   This is a good general hypothesis, but it gives no guide as to how to design the research experiment. The word *affect* is not measurable. How does it affect a person?

2. The hypothesis must be narrowed down to give a little direction. *"Synthetic chemical fertilizers when used in growing apples affect a person's pulse."*

   Now this hypothesis is not really testable.

3. The final stage is to design an experiment where the results can be measured. This is called a testable hypothesis. A testable hypothesis measures both what you do and what will happen.

"A person's pulse increases when s/he eats an apple that have been grown with synthetic chemical fertilizer opposed to when eating a certified organically grown apple."

A more refined hypothesis: *"I hypothesize that 20 people's pulse who each eat a certified organic apple will stay the same compared to 20 people who each eat a chemically fed apple whose pulse will get faster."*

This is a **testable hypothesis** because specific variables have been established, and by measuring a person's pulse before and after eating chemically raised apples against people eating organically raised apples, the student can make a comparison.

Note: Not every question can be answered by the scientific method. Only when you have a testable hypothesis can you use the scientific method to answer the question.

Now it is your turn. Have patience with the process. Take out your **Variables & Hypothesis Worksheet** and write your hypothesis. It may take you a few days to get it right.

When I was in graduate school, we were given 2 weeks to write our hypothesis. Our professor kept asking us to refine our hypothesis statement until it was testable.

Hypothesis Outcomes Checklist
Print the checklist, label its name, check off all the tasks you have completed and don't move on until all are checked! Attach it to your Science Log and date the entry.

I have written an excellent Hypothesis because....	✓
My hypothesis is based on information from my Background Research paper.	
My hypothesis consists of an independent and dependent variable.	
I have stated the hypothesis so that it can be tested in the experiment.	
I wrote a fair test.	

Let's call it a day. Job well done! Go outside and do something that is fun…

Make an appointment with your teacher so she can approve your hypothesis. Then a quick meeting with your parent(s) and you will be on your way to having an exciting day because you are going to design your science fair project experiment.

Meet With Your Teacher Again
Letter "O" on the Timeline

Make an appointment with your teacher. Bring your **Science Log**, worksheets and **Proposal Form** that you printed. Fill out the form before your meeting.

Here are some questions to discuss:
1. Can my project be completed within the time allotted?

2. What will be the estimated cost of completing the project?
    -   Do I need special equipment such as a microscope, slides or test tubes?
    -   Can the school supply some of the supplies needed?
    -   What supplies will I need? Add the supplies to your Supply List.

3. Is the design of the experiment effective?

4. Are the effects measurable in an objective way?

5. Does the project violate any state or federal laws pertaining to scientific research?

Ask your teacher to approve your variables and hypothesis. If necessary, tweak your writing.

After the appointment, in your Science Log, write a brief note about what happened at the meeting and what was decided. Tape or staple your hypothesis worksheet and proposal form in your Science Log. Be sure to date your entry.

IV - Testing Your Hypothesis

Write an Experimental Procedure
Letter "N" on the Timeline

I don't know about you, but I have been waiting for this day. This is the *reeeally fun* part of the investigation. Do you know why? Because this is the heart of your investigation. It is the action part. Read this section before you take action.

Types of Experiments
o **Natural Experiments/Quasi-Experiments** – involves making a prediction or forming a hypothesis and then gathering data by observing a system. The variables are not controlled in a natural experiment. Example: Children's long-term development when raised in foster care compared to those raised in families who adopted them.

o **Laboratory/Controlled Experiments** – lab experiments are controlled experiments, although you can perform a controlled experiment outside of a lab setting. In a controlled experiment, you compare an experimental group with a control group. Ideally, these two groups are identical except for one variable, the independent variable.

o **Field Experiments** – may be either a natural experiment or a controlled experiment. It takes place in a real-world setting, rather than under lab conditions. For example, an experiment involving an animal in its natural habitat would be a field experiment.

Errors in a Measurement
A Simple Explanation for High School Students
SECRET FILES #8

Definitions
All experimental uncertainty is due to either random errors or systematic errors.

o **Random errors** in experimental measurements are caused by unknown and unpredictable changes in the experiment. These changes may occur in the measuring of instruments or in the environmental conditions.

Random errors can be evaluated through statistical analysis and can be reduced by averaging over a large number of observations.

Examples of causes of random errors
- electronic noise in the circuit of an electrical instrument

- irregular changes in the heat loss rate from a solar collector due to changes in the wind

Systematic errors in experimental observations usually come from measuring instruments.

Systematic errors are difficult to detect and cannot be analyzed statistically because all of the data is off in the same direction (either too high or too low). Spotting and correcting for systematic error take a lot of care.

Examples of systematic errors
- there is something wrong with the instrument or its data handling system

- the instrument is wrongly used by the experimenter

Examples of systematic errors caused by the wrong use of instruments are:
- errors in measurements of temperature due to poor thermal contact between the thermometer and the substance whose temperature is to be found

- errors in measurements of solar radiation because trees or buildings shade the radiometer

  The **accuracy of a measurement** is how close the measurement is to the true value of the quantity being measured. The accuracy of measurements is often reduced by systematic errors, which are difficult to detect even for experienced research workers.

Note that systematic and random errors refer to problems associated with making measurements. *Mistakes* are made in the calculations or in reading the instrument *are not considered in error analysis*. It is assumed that the experimenters are careful and competent!

Look at the chart on the next page to learn how to minimize errors of measurement.

Examples of How to Minimize Experimental Error

Type of Error	Example	How to Minimize It
Random Errors	You measure the mass of a ring three times using the same balance and get slightly different values: 17.46g, 17.42 g, 17.44g	Take more data.
	Using a 100-millileter graduated cylinder to measure 2.5 milliliters of solutions	Equipment used to make the measurements is not sensitive enough.
Systematic Errors	The cloth tape measure that you use to measure the length of an object had been stretched out from years of use. (As a result, all the length measurements were too small.)	How would you compensate for the incorrect results of using a stretched-out tape measure?
	The electronic scale you use reads 0.05 too high for all your mass measurements (because it is improperly tared throughout your experiment).	How would you correct the measurements from improperly tared scale?
	Using a 1-quart milk carton to measure 1-liter samples of milk.	The volume would always be too small because a quart is slightly smaller than a liter.

Tips on How to Do an Excellent Experiment
The following details will contribute to an outstanding experiment, Project Report, and exhibit.

1. Write a numbered step-by-step procedure to test your hypothesis; include the steps you are going to take to set up your experiment and what must be done during an observation.

2. Take your time… don't rush…

3. Leave enough time so you can repeat your science experiment at least two more times. The more times the better. This helps to verify that your findings (results) were not a fluke.

   Surveys: Before you use a survey, check with your science fair rules to see if this type of investigation is allowed. You do not need to do your experiment 3 times if you are testing groups, but you do need a sufficient number of subjects (people) in the group to make sure your findings are reliable.

SurveyMonkey (https://tinyurl.com/2p95w36v) has an online free calculator to determine how many participants you will need for your survey. Find out how you can sign up for a free account (.https://www.surveymonkey.com/.).

4. Take photographs, videos and/or draw pictures as your experiment progresses. You don't want to miss a thing. Remember I mentioned that the Judges just love photographs. AND… you will want to look back on them in years to come. If you do not have a digital camera or cell phone, purchase an inexpensive disposable one. Look at **Shopping List 2** for suggestions.

5. Every day observe, keep track of your findings in your Science Log. Date each entry.

6. Follow the safety rules when you conduct your experiment.

Details on Writing an Experimental Procedure
Letter "N" on the Timeline

Write a step-by-step experimental procedure for testing whether your hypothesis is true or false. This document has every exact detailed step described so that anyone could duplicate your experiment exactly as you conducted it.

1. Plan how you are going to change your independent variable. Determine how you are going to measure how the change affects the dependent variable.

   Remember we discussed the importance of conducting a "fair test"? To do this you can only change one factor and the rest of the variables remain the same. That way you will know if the change (independent variable) affected the dependent variables.

2. To ensure that your results are accurate (consistent) you must repeat your experiment at least 2 more times. Each of these experiments is called a **trial** or **run**.

   o State in your experimental procedure how many trials you plan on performing.

   o Read the How to do an Excellent Experiment on the previous page to learn more about doing an experiment with plants or conducting a survey.

3. To have an excellent experiment you will need to compare different groups of trials with each other. This guarantees that the changes you observed by the change in the independent variable are caused by the independent variable.

   For example, if you want to find out if plants grow taller with chemical fertilizer than just in water with no fertilizer, then the experimental group will only be fed chemical fertilizer. Now you can compare two groups, one fed chemical fertilizer and one fed no fertilizer.

There are two types of groups:

o A **control group** in a scientific experiment is a group separated from the rest of the experiment where the independent variable being tested cannot influence the results. This isolates the independent variable's effects on the experiment and can help rule out alternate explanations of the experimental results. In this instance, the control group would not be fed any fertilizer.

Controlled groups are not necessary to all scientific experiments. Controls are extremely useful where the experimental conditions are complex and difficult to isolate.

Controlled groups can also be separated into two other types: *positive* and *negative*.

▪ **Positive control groups** are groups where the conditions of the experiment are set to guarantee a positive result. This type of group can show the experiment is functioning properly as planned.

▪ **Negative control groups** are groups where the conditions of the experiment are set to cause a negative outcome.

o An **experimental group** in a scientific experiment is the group where the experimental procedures are performed.

The experimental group is where the actual experiment is taking place. The independent variable is tested on the group and the changes in the dependent variables are recorded. The experimental group would be fed the chemical fertilizer that are located on the porch of your house or apartment.

Some experiments are different than the plant example. Some groups of trials are performed at different values. For example, if you want to find out if there is more energy output from a wind turbine using different blade sizes, you could experiment with 2", 3" and 4" blades and measure the output with a multimeter. Now you are comparing different groups to each other rather than comparing them to one control group.

Think about the experiment you want to perform and decide whether it is like the plant example that requires a special group control, or like the wind turbine that does not.

Remember we discussed controlled variables in the section of this book, *How to Construct a Hypothesis*? We explained that controlled variables are variables that you do not want to change when you conduct your experiment.

Most experiments have a few controlled variables. In the wind turbine experiment you would want to make sure that the material and thickness of all the blades are the same. And that whatever you use to generate "wind" is the same each time you run a trial - for example, a hair dryer using warm air at the same speed.

Carefully designing your experimental procedure will help to insure an excellent science fair project. Take out your Science Log; write down all the details required for your project experiment, step-by-step.

Take out the **Experimental Procedure Checklist** printable. Use it as a guide to make sure you design an excellent experimental procedure.

Example
Let's say that you want to know if a person's pulse is affected by chemical fertilizer.

You grow lettuce in tap water (water taken from your sink) and not add any fertilizer to the water. This will be for the controlled group.

You also grow lettuce in tap water but feed it chemical fertilizer. This will be fed to the experimental group.

On the day of testing gather all the participants in a room and have each sit in a chair. It is important that you do not tell the participants anything about the experiment. Show them how to take their pulse. Have each of them record how many times their pulse beats in one minute.

Then have each participant in the control group eat 1 cup of the lettuce grown in just tap water. At the same time, have the people in the experimental group eat 1 cup of lettuce that was grown in tap water and fed chemical fertilizer.

Have the participants sit quietly with their eyes closed for 20 minutes; no TV, no reading, no music, no games, no talking or laughing. Just silence.

Forty minutes after the participants have eaten the lettuce, have them take their own pulse again and record it.

Do the same in another 20 minutes. Is there a difference? Have them record the results.

Do the same again in another 20 minutes. Have them record the results.

Experimental Procedure Outcomes Checklist

Print the checklist. After all your items listed below are accomplished, attach the checklist to your Science Log. Date the entry.

I have an excellent Experimental Procedure because….	✓
I wrote my hypothesis. My variables are measurable.	
I wrote a detailed description and size for all control and experimental groups.	
I wrote a step-by-step list for all my procedures in detail.	
I described in detail how I am going to change the independent variable and how to measure that change.	
I explained in detail how I am going to measure the resulting change in the dependent variable / variables.	
I listed all the controlled variables.	
I explained how I am going to keep the controlled variables at a constant value.	
I declared how many times I am going to repeat the experiment, keeping in mind that 3 is the minimum, and that the number of repetitions is sufficient to give you reliable data.	
My experiment can be replicated exactly as I am going to do it because I wrote a very clear, precise, step-by-step experimental procedure.	

Move on to the next sections

Materials List
Letter "M" on the Timeline

Overview
The Materials Supply List is different than the shopping list. The Materials list is only for those items that you will need to do your experiment. The Experimental Procedure includes both the Materials List and the Procedure. This list will be included in the Experimental Procedure section of your Project Report that you will write after you have completed your experiment.

Materials List Example
The following is an example of a materials list for making bio-ethanol fuel from rice and tofu waste that was done by 3 twelve-year-old students from Indonesia.

Tools
3 empty places for the waste
Filter
Spoon
Tins
Distillation tools
Alcohol meter

Materials
Tofu waste
Cooked rice waste
Inoculum (Yeast)
Water
Plastics

How can the above list be improved so that others could replicate the same experiment?
- o 3 empty places for the waste - What specific kind of places? Are they referring to a hole in the ground or a container? What size container or place? What material is the container made of?
- o Filter – What material is it made of? Size? Shape? Manufacturer?
- o Spoon – What size and kind of spoon?
- o Tins – What kind of tins? Size, Shape? Are they plain tins or painted on the inside?
- o Distillation Tools – Name of each tool. Who is the manufacturer of the tools? Model number of each tool? Where measurable they purchased?
- o Alcohol meter – Manufacturer? Model number? Size (if relevant).
- o Tofu waste – Definition and explanation of tofu waste? How is the tofu waste made? Where did they get it? Did they make it? How much did they use in pounds or ounces?
- o Cooked rice waste – same questions as tofu waste.
- o Inoculum (Yeast) – How much yeast? Did they make the yeast or did they purchase it? If purchased, what is the brand name?
- o Water – How much water? What kind of water – tap, distilled, spring, etc.?
- o Plastics – What kind of plastics? Size? Shape? Dimensions? Name of type of plastics? Manufacturer? Model number?

Details of How to Make Your Materials List
Good cooks have all their ingredients assembled before they begin. A student "cooking" up a science fair project also needs to have all supplies and equipment on hand. That's why it's so important to create a list of everything you'll need before you start your experiment.

Some items will be easy to obtain. Others will require a little shopping, either at a store in your neighborhood or on a website. It's frustrating to have to stop in the middle of a project because of some item you forgot. And some items will need to be mailed to you. Leave enough time to receive materials, do your experiment 3 to 5 times, and meet the assignment's deadline.

Make your Materials Supply List as detailed and specific as you can because another scientist must be able to duplicate your experiment.

Take out the shopping list you have been keeping while deciding upon your topic and doing your background research. Remember you put it in your Science Log for safe keeping? Add all the materials and equipment you will need to do your experiment. Now add this list to **Shopping List 2** listed in the TOC.

Equipment, hospitals, high schools, community colleges, universities, manufacturers or your science teacher sometimes will allow you to use equipment under supervision. If your parent(s) or teacher do not have contacts at one of these institutions, then ask your parent(s) to help you network to find someone who does. If a doctor or scientist is interested in your project, they may also mentor you. Don't be shy, ask around. It will be worth the effort.

Ask a parent to accompany you while you make your purchases. It is illegal to use a charge card and sign for the purchases if you are not 18 years or older.

Materials List Outcomes Checklist
Print the checklist. Check off each item that you have completed. Do not go to the next section until you can check off all 6 items. Then attach the checklist to your Science Log, date the entry.

I Wrote an excellent Materials Supply List because...	✓
I listed every single item that I need to do my experiment.	
I listed the measurement of each item on the list (size, millimeter, centimeter, ounces, pounds, etc.).	
I described the materials I am going to use in enough detail so that the experiment can be duplicated exactly as I do it. (materials, brand of item, manufacturer, etc.)	
I entered all the above in my Science Log.	
I added the list of materials and equipment to Shopping List 2.	
I attached this page to my Science Log and dated the entry.	

3rd Meeting with Your Teacher & Parent(s)
Letter "L" on the Timeline

Get your teacher and parent(s) approval before you perform your experiment.

Take out the **Proposal Worksheet** that you printed. You can quickly fill out the details by looking at all the checklist pages that you completed. If you do not have enough room to input all the information in each of the spaces, then use another sheet of paper and attach it to the form. Then you will have all the information you need for the discussion with your teacher and parent(s).

Bring the printed pages to these meetings:
o Materials List & Shopping List 2 List
o Experimental Procedure
o Proposal Worksheet
o Your smile and enthusiasm
o Excellent listening skills.

After both meetings have been completed and you have approval from your teacher and a parent, it is time to go shopping.

If You Plan to Enter a Big/Top Fair

Now is the time to mail in your application. Each of the fairs has its own criteria so go to the websites to get the information and application.

In the Appendix of this book is a list of fairs. Choose the fair(s) that you want to enter.

If you have never been to a top fair, look in the Appendix to see what they look like. Prepare yourself… it is a huge event in a very large auditorium.

Shopping List 2

3-Ring Notebook with at least one pocket on the inside of the front cover. It will be used to store your Project Report and place on your table at the fair. Coordinate the color of the folder with your display board colors. (https://amzn.to/1PvfMtj)

1 - box of 3-ring clear Economy Weight **Sheet Protectors**
They are used to protect your Project Report pages from tearing or ink smearing when Judges, teachers and others read your report. (https://amzn.to/1PvftyB)

Tabbed Dividers
See Shopping List 1 if you have not purchased them already. Used to separate sections of your Project Report (.https://amzn.to/2Y0Cc4k.)

White Computer Paper (https://amzn.to/1MZLVar)
Used to print your Project Report and pages that go on your display board.

Computer Ink Cartridges (https://amzn.to/1SGvya1)
You want to make sure that your printer prints sharp fonts and images.

Display Boards (https://amzn.to/1Pvgtmh)
Look on the page of this book that shows you how to do an outstanding display board before you order any materials. A Teacher's Store in your neighborhood will have tri-fold boards. Walmart, Target, Blicks and Amazon.com are other possibilities.

Elmer's size tri-fold display boards are 36" x 48" for school fairs. Do not purchase a flimsy board because it will keep on falling down. Elmer's Tri-fold is the best quality board. You can get one that is corrugated cardboard or foam. They come in white and in an assortment of colors. (https://amzn.to/3MmdD8I)

Companion Board Stand

If you are going to do a complicated project or are going to attend a top science fair, it is a wise to do a Companion Board that will help you to summarize key points. It gives you the ability to explain a complex project to a judge / judges who probably will not know the intricacies of your project. The board stand will hold a 20" x 30" flat board. How to make a companion board is discussed later on in this book. (https://amzn.to/3fRSi6x)

Header Boards for Display Boards

Helps your board to stand out in the crowd and gives you more room to put a unique title for your display board. It sits at the top of your display board. Choose one that is manufactured by the same company so that it inserts securely. The header also helps the tri-fold board to not tip over. (https://amzn.to/3wsOBOn)

Construction Paper

Use color construction paper to place behind your printed material. It will act as a border for the sections of your report. Choose only one color.
Input link into your browser for color options. https://tinyurl.com/y7um9rbm)

Adhesives

Do not use Elmer's liquid glue because it will cause the paper to pucker. Rubber cement is a better choice. Here are more professional options.

- Dual Tip Glue Pen(https://tinyurl.com/ybxvnspa)
- Glue Stick (https://tinyurl.com/yadw3vgn)
- Spray Adhesive (https://tinyurl.com/yc3bo7sb)
- Mounting Tape (https://tinyurl.com/ychvkb9s)

Materials for Title Tags and Border

The following materials make your board look professional and stand out at the science fair. Self-adhesive repositionable letters are the best, but if you cannot afford them, then use a stencil and construction paper or dual color markers.

Letters & Numbers: (https://tinyurl.com/y7e7sxlj)

- Stencils: (https://tinyurl.com/y8pz9nmn)
- Markers: (https://tinyurl.com/ycx9xczd)
- Jumbo letters 4" high (https://tinyurl.com/yakxts63)
- Self-adhesive repositionable letters (https://amzn.to/39ogdMF)
- Repositionable adhesive (https://amzn.to/3KnbkkS)
- Repositionable borders (https://amzn.to/2Yp0uoJ)
- Borders (https://amzn.to/3uftclF)
- Jumbo Letters and Numbers (https://amzn.to/3weL33q)

In the chapter on how to make a display board, you will find the size lettering for each section of your board.

Photos

Plan to take photos of your equipment and supplies. Include them in your Project Report. Judges love photos. Do you remember the *Success is a Journey* story? It told you another important reason to take photos.

If you do not have a cell phone or digital camera, consider purchasing a disposable cell phone or disposable digital camera to take pictures.

Do Your Experiment
Letter "J" on the Timeline

Before You Begin Your Experiment
All professionals prepare before they begin their work. A detective does background information on the person or company he is investigating. The same is true with a scientist. Here is what you need to do before you begin your experiment.

- **Set up a place to work**. With your parent's permission, set up a special place in your home for your experiment. This place must be out of reach to siblings and/or pets. It is a permanent place that will not be needed by any member of the family until you are finished with your experiment.

  Arrange for a family meeting to explain the importance of your "hands off" policy.

- **Know what you are going to do in advance**. Read your experimental procedure until you know what to do for every step. If you have any questions or doubts then ask your parent or teacher to help clarify that step.

- **What to put in your workspace**.
  1. Experimental Procedure Checklist

  2. Science Log for taking notes and data table for collecting data.

  3. Arrange all the materials, equipment and supplies you will need to do your experiment so that they are easily accessible. If you are missing anything, now is the time to get it.

  4. **Be safe**.
     - Are you using equipment that is sharp or can hurt you? Then ask an adult to be present when you do your experiment or use dangerous equipment.

     - Use laboratory grade goggles, gloves and smock when necessary.

     - If your hair is long, make sure that you secure it in the back of your neck with a rubber band or hair band.

     - Do you need a fire extinguisher?

Conducting Your Experiment
Important Information

- Do you have your Science Log so that you can record all observations of your experiment? Your teacher will expect to read it and it is one of the key items that you place on your table at the science fair.

- Prepare a **data table** before you begin your experiment. The data table is where you are going to record your trials. We will show you how to make a data table in this chapter.
- Follow your Experimental Procedure exactly as you wrote it. If you make changes along the way, then you <u>must</u> document it in your experimental procedure and note the changes in your Science Log.

- Be accurate when you take measurements. If at all possible, numerical measurements are best.

- Take photos of every step that you perform of your experiment. You will be able to use them in your report and on your display board.

Recording Your Observations When Doing Your Experiment

It is not only important to take detailed notes and design excellent tables and charts, it is <u>a must</u> to record your observations in your Science Log as you are doing your experiment. Keep your records in order of occurrence.

Record the following
- Thought-provoking incidences

- Challenges or problems that happen

- Anything you change to the experimental procedure – if you do something different than what you planned

- New ideas that you have

- The unpredictable that occurs

All the above will be the foundation of your science fair project report which will include data, charts, graphs, conclusions and photos. You will be telling all in this report, including your accidents, failures and successes.

Be very precise when you record the procedure and measurements. Use a metal measurer instead of a cloth or paper one. Paper or cloth stretches.

Label your drawings. If you take pictures, write down the time, date and subject of the picture.

Whenever possible, remember to use numerical values when reporting data. If your project has qualitative data (not numbers), take photos or draw a picture of what happens at every step of your experiment.

Some students find it helpful to do a practice run of their experiment, recording and showing the data to their teacher or mentor. That way they can make revisions, if necessary, before moving ahead with the experiment. It is normal to find things that you want to change or adapt. It's all part of the process.

If you do make changes, remember to record your practice run in your Science Log along with the changes to the experimental procedure and why you made the changes.

Helpful Tips
- o   The better observer you are, the better your Project Report.

- o   The more details the better.

- o   Don't get sloppy as you move through the days of doing your experiment. Neatly record <u>each step</u> in your Science Log.

- o   Sporadically, remind your family to stay away from your workspace.

- o   Keep chemicals and supplies locked up or out of reach.

- o   Keep it clean and organized.

- o   Most importantly, be safe.

V – Analyze Data & Draw Conclusions

Record and Interpret Data
Letter "I" on the Timeline

Data

Hi! Welcome back. Congratulations on completing the research and experiment phase of your science fair project.

The Results section of your Project Report is where you will tell your readers the actual numbers (or other data) that you got as you were doing the experiment.

What is data? Data are the facts or bits of information that come from observing and testing an experiment. Scientists often use graphs or tables to show their data and research findings. Data can be numbers or words.

The purpose of tables and graphs is twofold: 1) help you to analyze and interpret your results and 2) enhance the clarity of your experiment to a reader or viewer.

o   Use charts and graphs to express the data and patterns. Ask yourself:
   ▪ Did I get the results I expected?
   ▪ What can I learn from the results?

o   Always have a title for your tables and graphs. Place it at the top of the table or graph.

o   If you are a high school or college student and your experiment is with specific animals or plants, include the scientific and common name. Underline and put all scientific names in *italics*.

o   In your Project Report, you can include more than one data table, as long as the format is clear and easy to read.

o   Number the tables consecutively throughout your report.

o   Take time to think about what your data tells you.

This is a great site to see different types of testing and data analysis. Also included are abstracts and reports. Go to Nature.com (http://www.nature.com). Scroll down on the page to **Latest Research**. Or go to the top of the page and click on "Search". A window will appear on your left. Insert the word your category of science.

How to Organize Data

You don't know if you prove or disprove your hypothesis unless you collect data. Don't get so involved in doing your experiment that you forget to collect and record your data.

Tables

Organize the results of your experiment on easy-to-read tables. A table organizes data into **rows** and **columns**.

> **Rows** go across
> **Columns** go up and down.
> **Headings** tell you what each column of data represents, in this case the 'trip' number and types of trash ('plastic', 'glass', 'styrofoam', and 'cigarettes'.

Example of a Table

A class made 5 trips to the beach to collect the trash left on the sand. Question: Which type of trash makes up the biggest part or portion of all the trash? To do this we want to look at the totals for each type of trash.

What does the intersecting green box tell you? The intersecting green box gives the number of plastic pieces (given by *column heading*) collected on trip 2 (given by *row heading*).

Trip	Plastic	Glass	Styrofoam	Cigarettes
1	43	11	38	139
2	108	5	59	314
3	55	5	24	122
4	69	7	52	167
5	174	3	100	504

Types of Graphs

You can use graphs to express the results of your data. They are pictures that help us to understand amounts. These can be drawn on graph paper or on your computer. Here are different types of graphs:

There are picture graphs and histograms, but for your science fair project, choose from one of the graphs listed on the following pages. .

Bar Graph

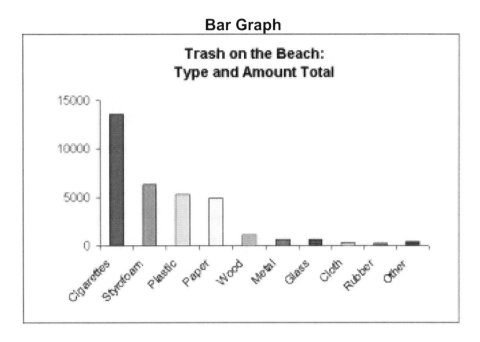

Trash on the Beach:
Type and Amount Total

How different are these variables to each other?

Bar graphs are great for looking at differences amongst similar things. In this case we are comparing types of trash. Bar graphs are good for giving a comparison of absolute numbers. This is a useful graph for determining the actual amounts of each type of trash.

Bar graphs are also excellent because you can stack numbers of things right next to each other and compare them instantly. The height of each stack can tell you the number of each type of trash that is found on the beach, either approximately, by the numbers on the vertical axis, or exactly, by labeling each stack with the exact number.

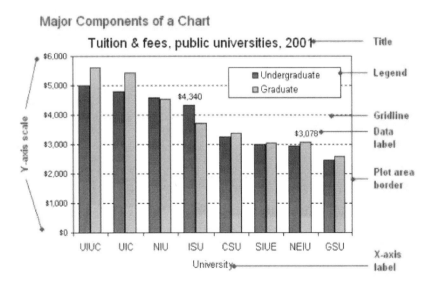

Major Components of a Chart

Tuition & fees, public universities, 2001

However, if we wanted to compare what portion each stack may represent of all the trash combined, we need a pie graph.

Pie Graph

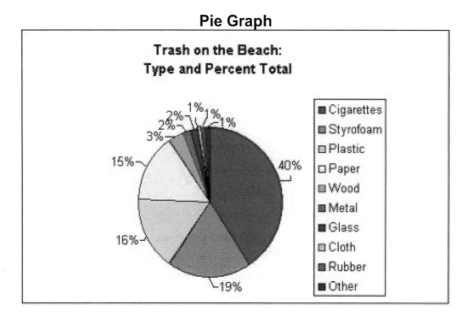

Trash on the Beach:
Type and Percent Total

Legend:
- Cigarettes
- Styrofoam
- Plastic
- Paper
- Wood
- Metal
- Glass
- Cloth
- Rubber
- Other

Values: 40%, 1%, 1%, 1%, 2%, 2%, 3%, 15%, 16%, 19%

What portion of the total does each part make up?

A pie graph allows us to compare parts of the whole with each other, or the fraction of the whole each part takes up. That might sound a bit complicated, but it's easy when you think about it in terms of cake.

You're starting to pick up some real science smarts! Pie graphs represent data in a visual, easy to read manner, which helps us to understand data more clearly. Using this pie graph, we can see what portion of all the trash each particular type of trash represents (how big of a piece of cake each type of trash "eats"). It's as simple as that!

Even though graphs can look simple, there's a lot of information in a graph.

Let's say you eat half of the cake (Boy, you were hungry!), how much of the cake is left? (50%) Obviously if you ate one side of the cake, then the other side is still there. Let's say you weren't quite so hungry, so you only ate half of that half. (25%) How much is left of the cake now?

You get the idea. The most you could ever possibly eat is the whole cake (100%), because after that, there's no more cake left! The less you eat of the cake, the more you have left over.

Now consider two categories of trash: wood and plastic. Let's say that they were the only two types of garbage found. If half the total garbage we find is wood, then plastic must also be half the garbage found. But is it possible that half of the garbage is wood IF more than half of it is plastic? NO WAY! That's the same thing as eating more than the whole cake! Once all the cake is gone, you can't eat anymore!!

Line Graph

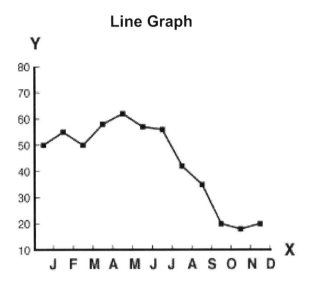

How Does This One Variable Change Over Time?

A line graph is used to show changes through time or space. Since we are not looking at changes through time and space this *is not* a useful graph type for the garbage experiment. But this type of graph may be needed to show your data, so let's learn about it.

For your science fair project, plot the independent variable on the X-axis and the dependent variable on the Y-axis.

Making a line graph is really just a matter of connecting the dots. Let's say we have data on dolphin (Y) sightings for a particular area. The data tells us the date (X) and the number of dolphins seen. In order to make a line graph we need consistent data. Let's go back over "consistency" after we get the general idea first.

First, let's make the dots. (J for January, F for February, M for March… and so forth.) We move (across) horizontally along the graph with the dates in order, and then (go up) vertically to the number of dolphins sighted for each date and make a dot.

Now we connect the dots. By connecting the dots, we suggest that the data points are related. In this case they are related through time, the number of dolphins sighted changes through time. Maybe time has an effect on the number of dolphins. For example, they could be seasonal, showing up in the winter and not the summer.

What did I mean by "we need consistent data?" Well, line graphs suggest a trend through time, so we might get the wrong trend if we don't have enough data.

Let's say we took sightings on the number of whales in a given area, but only took them before and after they actually migrated through the area. Well, if we connected all the dots, then we would give a flat line of zero numbers through the time when they were not present. This gives the wrong trend, and the whales would be left out. You don't want to hurt their feelings, do you?

Here is a free site where you can visually communicate your data into charts and graphs **NCES.Ed.gov** (https://tinyurl.com/ytc2cf3h) You have the option of selecting an area, bar, line, XY or pie graph.

If you have more than one set of data, show each series in a different color or symbol and include a legend with clear labels. Here is an example:

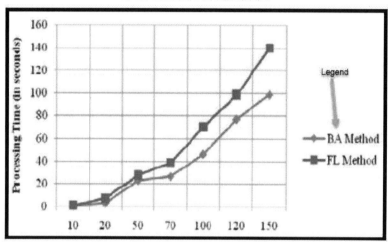

Boolean and Fuzzy Methods on Category A: AH1N1 DNA Sequences

What is a Data Table?

A data table is an organized arrangement of information in labeled rows and columns. It is a way to present and display information about a group of related facts. It is especially useful in recording observations made during a scientific investigation.

Organizing your results will allow you and those looking at your work to draw conclusions about the problem you are going to be investigating.

There are 2 steps to organizing the information or data that you gather:
1. Data Table
2. Make a graph from the data table.

How to Make Your Data Table
Now it is time to organize your table. Always give your table a title and label your rows and columns. You can use Excel or Word to create a table.

Template for Data Table

Independent Variable	Dependent Variable			Derived Quantity
	Trial 1	Trail 2	Trial 3	

Examples of Trial Data Tables

The pH of Common Household Substances

Substance	pH			Average pH
	Trial 1	Trial 2	Trial 3	
Lemon Juice	2.4	2	2.2	2.2
Baking Soda	8.4	8.3	8.7	8.5
Orange Juice	3.5	4	3.4	3.6

Example 2

Solubility Rate Experiment

Trial	Size of Crystals (mm)	Temperature (°C)
1	0.1 - 0.2	20
2	0.1 - 0.2	40
3	0.5 - 1.0	10
4	0.5-1.0	20

Tips on Recording Data
o Now it is time to review and record the data obtained from your science fair experiment.
  ▪ Did you include all your findings or do you need to add more data?
  ▪ Do you need to collect more data?
  ▪ Did you calculate everything correctly?

o Calculate an average for the different trials of your experiment, if you did more than one trial.

o Label all tables and graphs so if a stranger is looking at them s/he will know what the chart is about. Include the units of measurement (grams, inches, volts, etc.).

o Place your independent variable on the x-axis of your graph and the dependent variable on the y-axis.

o **Remember to record and keep everything in your Science Log.**

Experiment Outcomes Checklist
Print the checklist. Check off every single item that you completed. If you did not complete an item, then go back and do so. Attach the checklist in your Science Log, date the entry.

I have an excellent science fair Experiment because…	✓
I recorded in detail my observations in my Science Log.	
I recorded the data in a data table which I attached to my Science Log.	
I was careful and precise when I made my measurements.	
I made sure that my controlled variables remained constant so that they did not affect the results.	
I ran at least 3 trials.	
I recorded all changes I made to the experimental procedure (if any).	
I recorded all challenges or problems in my Science Log.	

Go on to the next section once you have checked off all the above items.

Analyzing Your Data
Letter "I" on the Timeline

Overview
In your Science Log, using your notes, tables, charts and graphs, analyze what happened in the science fair experiment.

Start with a summary of your science fair project results. Don't make it longer than a few sentences. Your summary will be the basis for the conclusion, which will state whether your results prove or disprove your original hypothesis.

In Your Conclusion Include the Following
o Data from your background research that helps explain the results of your experiment.

o Explain whether or not the data supports or calls in question your hypothesis. Accept or reject the hypothesis.

o State how the independent variable affected the dependent variable.
o State what the investigation showed. You could also provide comments about the experimental procedure, whether it was effective in proving or disproving your hypothesis.

o You may include other explanations, such as conditions that you were not able to control that may have affected the results.

o Make recommendations for changes to the experimental procedure, if any.
o Give one sentence, if any, as to what you would do differently next time.

Use Calculations to Analyze Your Data

When indicated, use a spreadsheet, like Microsoft Excel, to perform calculations on your raw data. The results will help you to form your conclusions. You can use the spreadsheet to show the results in your Project Report. Remember to label the rows and columns.

Do you recall that we suggested that you do at least one extra trial of your experiment? If you did as we suggested, you will have more extensive data.
o Use known formulas to perform your calculations and show the relationships you tested ($E = MC^2$, F = MA, V = IR)

o Keep all the units of measurement consistent. For example, L with L, mL with mL.

Data Analysis Outcomes Checklist

Print the following 2 checklists. Check off the items you completed. If you didn't complete an item, then do so. Attach the checklist to your Science Log and date the entry.

I made an excellent Data Chart because...	✔
I collected enough data to test my hypothesis.	
I made sure my data is accurate.	
When needed, I summarized the data with an average.	
I labeled rows and columns.	
My chart specifies units of measurement for all the data.	
I double checked to make sure that all calculations are correct.	

Only move on to the following checklist if you were able to check off each of the above statements.

Graph Outcomes Checklist

My Graph is Really Good Because....	✔
I used the correct type of graph to express the data.	
I gave each graph a title.	
I placed the independent variable on the x-axis and the dependent variable on the y-axis.	
I labeled the axes correctly and specified the units of measurement.	
The graph has the appropriate high and low values on the axes.	
I plotted the data correctly and clearly.	

After you checked off all questions, take a break. You deserve it. Tomorrow we will move on to the next step.

Drawing Conclusions
Letter "H" on the Timeline

Details

Your conclusions are a summary. <u>It is the answer to your question</u>. It needs to be clear, concise and to the point. Resist the temptation to give your own interpretation or opinion. Simply stated, it tells whether the results of your science fair project prove or disprove your original hypothesis.

Take out your Science Log, using your notes, charts and graphs, analyze what happened as a result of your experiment.

Did your hypothesis hold up?
o   Did your results agree with your hypothesis? State what the investigation showed.

o   Accept or reject your hypothesis.

o   Include any relevant background research data that helps explain your results. If the results suggest a relationship between the independent and dependent variables, state what they were.

o   You may also want to include other explanations, such as conditions you were not able to control that may have affected the results.

If your results disprove your hypothesis, do not go back and make changes in the hope that you will come up with a different result. All you have to do is provide an explanation of why the events of your experiment did not conform to your expectations. This is part of the scientific process. And realize that you have already made big strides in your scientific knowledge.

Actually, professional scientists welcome unexpected results. They use them to construct a new hypothesis for a new experiment. Science Fair Judges care only about what you have learned, not whether you have proven your hypothesis or not.

If your hypothesis is not supported by your experiment, what additional experiments you might want to conduct.

Use your Science Log to jot down ideas and thoughts about the conclusions drawn. Write your conclusion in your Science Log.

Example of a Conclusion
Results
The experiment test shows that there is a significant difference in the properties of thermoplastic starch when you add Milkfish bone particles when testing for water absorption and tensile strength.

The composite did not fully overcome the properties of a commercially produced plastic, especially for those used in grocery stores when testing for its water absorption and tensile strength.

Conclusion
Therefore, I conclude that there is significant improvement in the properties of TPS when added with the milkfish bone particles.

Drawing Conclusions Outcomes Checklist

Print the checklist. Check off all items until they completed. Attach checklist to the Science Log, date the entry.

I wrote excellent Conclusions because...	✓
I summarized my results and used it to support the findings.	
My conclusions state whether or not my findings proved or disproved the findings.	
When indicated, I stated the relationship between the independent and dependent variable.	
I summarized and evaluated the experimental procedure. I made comments about its success and effectiveness.	
I suggested changes in the experimental procedure and/or possibilities or further study. I asked myself the question, "What would I do differently next time?"	

Now you can take a long break. Have a good night's sleep because you have a few BIG days ahead of you. You are actually going to write your science fair Project Report and Abstract. See you then....

VI - Communicating Results

Writing Your Project Report Paper
Letter "G" on the Timeline

Overview
What is a Science Fair Project Report Paper?

○ A summary that answers the research question you wrote when you did your background research.

○ A review all of your references you consulted in searching for those answers including written publications, Internet resources, and interviews with experts.

○ A way to impress the judges by showing them how well you understand the results of and the theory behind your experiment.

○ A communication to others that details what you did and possible research that they can do to improve upon your findings. It is the write-up of your research and experiment.

There are 3 steps to finishing your science fair report:
1. What is the most efficient way to write your project report paper?
Use your **Complete Science Fair Project Checklist** and **Timeline** because they will give you an easy outline to follow. They show you from beginning to end every step you took to complete your project investigation.

Your Science Log will fill in all the details, including the data expressed in words, charts and tables.

2: This is where you write your science report with all the gory details!
But you say, "I'm not good at writing". Or, "I can't stand to write papers." Believe it or not, I use to freeze every time I had to look at a computer or paper to write even a sentence.

 #9
Don't worry about the writing. Just write whatever you know... after all, you ran the investigation and you were there every step of the way!

Keep in mind that your report needs to include every minute (mynoot) detail of your investigation so that your experiment can be duplicated. If someone read your report and knew nothing about the project, they would be able to experience all the details of your investigation as if they did it themselves.

After you write the report, go back and fix it up. And remember to have someone edit your report... more on that later.

3: Once your report is written it is time to write an abstract.

What is an abstract? It is a brief, written discussion of your science fair project. We will later discuss what sections to include and how to write one.

Let's move on to writing your science fair project report...

Tips for Your Project Report

This time you are writing the details of your report. Would you believe that you are getting down to the wire of bringing this mystery to a close?

Do you know the saying…

If you think you can, you can.
And if you think you can't, you're right!
Mary Kay Ash, Founder of Mary Kay Cosmetics

 #10

Well, I think – you think – you can because you have. And that's what counts the most... what YOU feel, think and believe.

Enough chatter. Let's move on…..

Before you write your report, check with your teacher regarding your school's rules and guidelines. It precedes anything we recommend.

1. Your report will most likely be long. Chunk this section into bite-size pieces, doing a little bit every day. It may take you up to a week or two to complete the whole report. Using a word processor makes it much easier than writing it by hand.

2. Check your ink cartridges (http://amzn.to/1kAhsd5). Make sure that they are full. You will want to use various colors to make your charts, tables and graphs. If you need to replenish your supply, now is the time to purchase them.

3. About every 5 minutes save your document. You don't want any of your work to be lost if all of a sudden there is a glitch with your computer. At the end of the day make a copy of your document in case one gets corrupted. Time is precious and you don't want to waste it.

4. Use spell and grammar check at the end of every day. As you finish a day's work, print it out and read it. Make any changes on the paper. Then give it to one of your parents or older siblings and ask them to write suggestions in the margin. The next day, input your changes before you begin writing the new material.

Organization and Sections of Your Project Report

o The Title Page – page 1 of your report. In the center of the page write the Project Title, your name, grade, school and date. Some schools want only the Title of your project on the first page. Write the title so it grabs the reader's attention. Do not make it the same as your Big Question.

o Table of contents - page 2 of your report. Include a page number in front of the name of each section. Center the word "Content" or "Table of Contents" at the top of the page. Number the sections of the report in a list below the TOC. If you know how to generate a TOC automatically, it is the most accurate way to formulate it.

Table of Contents
Abstract
Introduction
Big Question
Background Research
Experimental Procedure
Materials List
Data Analysis & Discussion
Conclusion
Ideas for Future Research
Acknowledgements
Bibliography

o **Abstract** - a brief overview of the project - one or two paragraphs. No more than one page. Write the Abstract last because then you will have an overview of what your project was about.

o **Introduction** - explanation of what prompted your research and what you hoped to achieve. In other words, state what is the purpose of your paper.

o **Big Question** – a specific scientific question that is answered by the results of your science fair experiment.

o **Background Research** - this is the research paper you wrote before you did your experiment.

o **Materials List** - lists all the materials and supplies you used for your experiment.

o **Experimental Procedure** - describe in detail the method used. Be sure to explain every detail so that someone could repeat the experiment step by step. This is where you include your photos.

o **Data Analysis & Discussion** - include all data and measurements from your experiment along with drawings, charts and graphs. The discussion explains the results and is a summary of what you discovered during your observations, from your data table(s) and graph(s). Compare your results with published data you found in your research.

If you have extensive data that is several pages, put it in an appendix at the back of your notebook. If it is very long put it in another binder, write a summary statement along with the data.

- **Conclusion** – results and conclusion obtained from your experiment.
  - Compare your results with published data you found in your research.

  - Possible ways in which the project could be expanded or improve upon.

  - Suggest an alternative experiment if the results did not support your hypothesis.

  - Only include what was stated earlier in the paper.

- **Ideas for Future Research** - Some schools want to know what you would do differently if you repeated the experiment or possible ways in which the project could be expanded in the future.

- **Acknowledgements** - brief statement stating the names of people who helped you and thanking them for their contribution to your success.

- **Bibliography** - Books, magazines, journal, articles, Internet websites, and interviews that you used to do your research. Ask each person's permission that you interviewed to print their name, title, work address and work phone number. Be sure that each source you cite in your paper appears in your bibliography.

Formatting Your Paper

Remember we discussed MLA and APA guidelines in the Bibliography? Ask your teacher what format to follow and if she wants to change any of the formatting guidelines as listed below. Show her this list.

	APA Guidelines	MLA Guidelines
Paper		8.5" x 11" (standard size in U.S.
Page Margins	1" (top, bottom left, right)	1" (top, bottom left, right)
Font Size	12 pt. Times Roman or Courier. Figures: Arial	12 pt. (Times, Roman, Arial, Calibri)
Line Spacing	Double-spaced	Double-spaced (include captions and bibliography)
Alignment of Text	Flush left with an uneven right margin	Flush left with an uneven right margin
Paragraph Indentation	5 to 7 spaces	½" (or 5 spaces)
End of Sentence	Leave 1 line space after a paragraph unless your teacher wants 2 spaces.	Leave 1 line space after a paragraph unless your teacher wants two.
Page Numbers	On all pages, ½" (except Figures) from top of right margin and flush with the right margin, 2 or 3 words of the paper's title (called the running head) and 5 spaces to the left of the page number, beginning with the Title Page. Example: Student's Guide to 1	On all pages, ½" from top of right margin and flush with the right margin. Put your last name followed by the number. Example: Binder 1
Title Page	The Title Page is the 1st page of your report. The running head is flush left in all upper-case letters, following the words, "Running Head". Example: Running Head: TITLE OF YOUR PAPER Below the running head, center the following on their own lines, using upper- and lower-case letters: Paper Title Your Name Your school	On the 1st page in the upper left corner, on separate lines, double-spaced: Your Name Teacher's Name Course Name or Number Date Underneath, center the title of your Project Report using regular title capitalization rules and no underline.

Section Headings	On the page center Level 1 headings, using upper- and lower-case letters. Place Level 2 headings flush left, italicized, using upper- and lower-case letters. Example: Communicating Results (Level 1) *Writing Your Final Report* (Level 2)	
Tables, Diagraphs, Illustrations and Photos	Place tables and Illustrations at the end of your paper. Each table is placed on a separate piece of paper, typed flush left on the 1st line below the page number. Double-space the table title flush left (italicize the letters using uppercase and lowercase letters). Example: *Table* 1 Place figure captions on the last numbered page of the report. The label figure is italicized and the caption is not. The caption uses regular sentence capitalization. The figures follow, one per page.	Sources and notes appear below the table, illustration or photo, flush left. Label the table, *Table*. Number the tables in numerical order: Table 1 Place the table label and caption above the table, Capitalize like a title, flush left. Photos, illustrations, charges, graphs or diagrams are labeled Figure or Fig., labeled in numerical order: Fig. 1 The label, title and source (when there is one) is placed beneath the figure, flush left, in a continuous block of text, not on a separate line:
Order of Major Sections	Each section begins on a new page: Title Page Footnotes Abstract Tables Body Figure Captions References Figures Appendixes	
Binding		Ask your teacher what s/he prefers. (staple, paper clip or placed in a 3-ring binder)

First Draft

Your report is the written expression of all your work.

Letter "F" on the Timeline

o   Write a first draft of your science fair project report. A first draft is the first time you write your report. Include the following:
- Introduction
- Big Question
- Background Research
- Hypothesis
- Experimental Procedure
- Materials List
- Numbered step-by-step explanation of your experimental procedure
- Analysis of data results leading to the conclusion
- Conclusion
- Ideas for Future Research
- Acknowledgments
- Bibliography

o   When possible, use a computer to write your report. Double space your lines.

o   Create data charts, graphs, tables and pictures. Use the spell check to edit and revise your report.

o   You are going to want to reference your sources of information and quotes. Go to https://www.youtube.com and do a search: how to input footnotes in a word document.

o   Ask someone who has excellent writing skills to edit for grammar, clarity and spelling.

2nd Draft

Letter "F" on the Timeline

After the 1st draft is edited, input suggested changes. Give this revision to the editor to proofread the paper again.

Final Copy

Letter "E" on the Timeline

When you are satisfied with the results, type a revised, polished copy for the final report. Be sure to spell check this final copy.

o   Print your final copy, on only one side of the paper, on clean white paper.
o   Place each sheet of paper in a 3-ring, clear protector (see Shopping List 2).

○ Put all the protected papers of your report in a 3-ring notebook that has a pocket. (see Shopping List 2) This notebook will be handed in to your teacher and placed on your display table at the science fair.

Project Report Outcomes Checklist #1

Do not stop working on this section until you can truthfully check off the above statements. After all sections have been completed, print and attach the checklist to your Science Log. Date the entry!

Once you have finished writing your Project Report, put it aside for a few hours or even a day. You want to read it again with "fresh eyes". Any deficiencies will become clear to you based on these criteria:

I did an excellent Project Report Paper because....	✓
I defined all important terms.	
I answered all my research questions.	
My background research helped me to make an educated guess (hypothesis) of what would happen in my experiment.	
I understand the reasons the behavior I observed as it occurred.	
I have included math that helped me to interpret my data.	
Credit was given to all the sources that I used. All copied phrases, sentences or paragraphs are in quotations.	
I recorded in my Science Log the experts that I interviewed and what I learned from each interview.	

Writing Your Abstract
What is a Science Fair Project Abstract?
Letter "D" on the Timeline

Overview
The purpose of an abstract is to give the reader an overview of your project so that s/he can decide whether or not to read the entire report. Get the reader excited and motivated to read your Abstract.

○ An abstract is a brief, written discussion of your project.

○ Each abstract consists of a brief statement of the essential, or most important, thoughts about your project. Abstracts summarize, clearly and simply, the main points of the experiment and/or the main sections of the report.

○ Syntax, spelling, grammar, punctuation, neatness, and originality are important.

○ Each student who does a science fair project must write an abstract that will be displayed with their project.

- Some science fair project abstracts are placed on the table in a folder while others are attached to the display board. Follow your school's guidelines.

- Think of your abstract as the "coming attractions" for a movie. If your abstract is interesting enough, people will be excited to read your final Project Report.

Details

Explaining your science fair project in an abstract of 250 words can be a challenge, and many students actually find it easier to write the long final report. Yet the abstract is a critical part of your science fair project.

It appears at the beginning of your final report, and also on the display board or table at the science fair. It's a summary that tells the reader what your project is all about.

5 Sections of Your Abstract
1. Project title
2. Purpose of your project
3. Hypothesis
4. Description of the procedure
5. Results
6. Conclusions

It may also include any possible research applications.

Write a very brief explanation of each:
1. Introduction - **Purpose of Your Project**
   Why You Undertook the Project
   Something motivated you to explore a hypothesis. Was it an observation you made, a question that occurred to you, a frustration you experienced with some aspect of daily life? Let the reader into your head.

   Write an introductory statement of the reason for investigating the topic of your project.

2. **A Statement of the Hypothesis Being Studied**
   A single clear statement is all that's needed.

3. **Procedures Used - What You Did**
   - Overview / summary of the key points of your investigation. Include the variables you selected.

   - Only include procedures that you, the student, did.

   - Do not include work done by a mentor, acknowledgements, work done by a university lab or work done prior to your involvement in your project.

- Do not give details about the materials used unless it greatly influenced the procedure or had to be developed to do the investigation.

4. Observation/Data/Results - What You Discovered
- State the key results that led directly to the conclusions you have drawn. What contribution did you make in completing this project? Were your objectives met?

- Do not give too many details about the results nor include tables or graphs.

5. Conclusions - What It Means?
- Describe briefly conclusions that you derived from your investigation.

- In the summary paragraph, reflect on the process and possibly state some applications and extensions of the investigation.

Look at the Abstract Template on the next page.

110

Abstract Template

Print and save this page.

Do not use bullet points in your abstract. They are written below to give you directions. Remember you only have 250 words, which does not include the Title, Your Name or School Name.

The different colors in the abstract demonstrates the following concepts. Do not use the colors in your Abstract:

Title Name School
Purpose of Experiment Write a statement telling the purpose of your experiment. An introductory statement of the reason for investigating the topic of the project. State your hypothesis.
Procedures Used Summarize procedures, emphasizing the key points of each step. A summarization of the key points and an overview of how the investigation was conducted. Omit details about the materials used unless it greatly influenced the procedure or had to be developed to do the investigation. An abstract must only include procedures done by the student. Work done by a mentor (such as a surgical procedure) or work done prior to student involvement must not be included.
Observations/Data/Results Very briefly detail observations / data / results. Only write the key results that lead directly to the conclusions you have drawn. Don't give too many details about the results nor include graphs or charts.
Conclusions State conclusions / applications. The summary paragraph must only reflect on the process and possibly state some applications and extensions of the investigation. An abstract does not include a bibliography unless specifically required by your local fair. The Intel ISEF requires the bibliography as part of the research plan to be provided on Form 1A.

(Cole, Mastering the Writing Process)

Sample Abstract

Effects of Marine Exhaust Water on Algae
Jones, Sally C.
High School, Hometown, IA

This project in its present form is the result of bioassay experimentation on the eff **of two-cycle marine engine exhaust water on certain green algae.** The initial idea to determine the toxicity of outboard engine lubricant. Some success with lubric eventually led to the formulation of "synthetic" exhaust water which, in turn, led to use of actual two-cycle engine exhaust water as the test substance.

Toxicity was determined by means of the standard bottle or "batch" bioassay techni Scenedesmus quadricauda and Ankistrodesmus sp. were used as the test organis Toxicity was measured in terms of a decrease in the maximum standing crop. effective concentration - 50% (EC 50) for Scenedesmus quadricauda was found t 3.75% exhaust water; for Ankistrodesmus sp. 3.1% exhaust water using the b technique.

Anomalies in growth curves raised the suspicion that evaporation was affecting results; therefore, a flow-through system was improvised utilizing the characteristic a device called a Biomonitor. Use of the Biomonitor lessened the influenc evaporation, and the EC 50 was found to be 1.4% exhaust water using Ankistrodes sp. as the test organism. Mixed populations of various algae gave an EC 50 of 1.: exhaust water.

The contributions of this project are twofold. First, the toxicity of two-cycle ma engine exhaust was found to be considerably greater than reported in the litera (1.4% vs. 4.2%). Secondly, the benefits of a flow-through bioassay technique utili the Biomonitor were demonstrated.

(Cole, Mastering the Writing Process)

Abstract Writing & Revising Tips

o   The abstract is printed on one page and is usually between 100 to 250 words for grades 4 through 12, and 50 to 250 words for grades 3. (Check your school for their guidelines.)

o   **Revise and edit the abstract**. To write only 250 words, first write a draft of the abstract. Then go back and cross out all extraneous words, phrases and sentences. Combine sentences together. Take a break and go over the abstract a couple hours later or the next day. The finished abstract will only be the "bare bones" of your report.

- Include the Project Title, School Name, City, State and Grade Level.

- To keep to the 250-word limit, each of these points needs to be covered in only a sentence or two. However, in your first draft, just write down your thoughts without worrying about the word count. Your second (or third, or fourth) draft is for strengthening your sentences and improving word choices.

  - Focus on these points: purpose (hypothesis), methods, scope, results, conclusions, and recommendations.

  - Do not include any mentor or supervisor's work.

  - Leave out details and discussions.

  - Combine sentences and/or paragraphs. You will probably edit several times in order to shorten the sentences.

  - Delete words, phrases or sentences that do not add anything to what you've already stated.

  - Use short sentences but still vary the structure.

  - Eliminate jargon.

  - Write in the past tense, but, when necessary, use active verbs rather than passive verbs.

    > Examples:
    > Active verbs: clarified, reviewed, inspected
    > Passive verbs: is, was, has been

  - Use complete sentences. Do not abbreviate words or leave out small words.

  - Spell check for spelling grammar and punctuation.

  - Eliminate words that are too technical for most readers. Use scientific language when necessary.

- When explaining key points, focus on the current year's research and work you have done on your project in the past year or less.

- <u>Do not include</u> tables and graphs.

- Judges and the public must have an accurate idea of the project after reading the abstract. Yet, you want to grab the reader's interest because it will influence their attitude about your full Project Report when they review it.

Look at it like a trailer to a movie. Make it interesting and engaging. Have other's read it and give suggestions each time you revise your draft. Have other's read it and give suggestions each time to revise your draft.

o An abstract does not include a bibliography or citations unless specifically required by your local fair.

o The Intel ISEF requires the bibliography to be part of the research plan.

o <u>Neatly</u> fill out the science fair form that your school gave to you.

Abstract Outcomes Checklist

Print the following 2 checklists. For each checklist, check off all the items you accomplished. If you did not complete one, then do so. Then attach each list to your Science Log and date each entry.

I Included….	✓
A sentence or two introducing the reason for your project	
Your hypothesis statement	
The procedures you used	
The results you obtained	
The conclusions you drew	

I Eliminated….	✓
Terms that are too technical	
Jargon	
Unexplained acronyms	
Unnecessary repetition	
Bibliography or citations	
Tables or graphs	
Procedures done by scientist or mentor	

Now you can move on to the next page and complete the checklist.

Project Report Outcomes Checklists 2

Print and save this page.

I Included....	✓
Abstract I wrote a summary paragraph on each of the following sections: Hypothesis Procedures Results Conclusions	
Final Report I included in my final report all the following sections: Title Page Abstract Table of Contents Big Question Variables Hypothesis Background Research Experimental Procedure Materials List Data Analysis & Discussion – I included data table and graph(s). Conclusions Idea for Future Research Acknowledgments Bibliography	

I did the following.....	✓
I had someone other than I edit the Project Report (including Abstract).	
I typed / input the final copies of both abstract and report.	
I printed both the abstract and report using a computer printer or going to a quick print store?	
I placed each of the pages of the report in a 3-ring clear plastic protector.	
I placed all the protected sheets of the report in a 3-ring binder that matches one of the colors of my display board.	

Please, do not move on to the next section of this book until you have completed everything on the list that your school requires. Hang in there! You are in the home stretch!!! When you have checked off all the above outcomes, attach this page to your Science Log and date the entry.

Take a long-needed break. See you tomorrow when you begin doing your display board. Make sure you have all the necessary materials. If you like doing art and craft projects, you will have lots of fun.

Creating Your Display Board
Letter "C" on the Timeline

Overview
Did you know that your display board is the first impression that the Judges see? It is a display that tells the story of all your efforts. Keep it simple, very neat and well organized.

Rules are different for each school regarding sizes, shapes and material composition for the backboards / display boards / exhibit boards. Check with your school before purchasing materials.

Color Scheme
o   Before you purchase anything for your display board, decide on a color scheme. Do a search on the Internet on "how to use a color wheel". This will help you to choose your color scheme. It is best to not use more than three to five contrasting colors. Check to see your school's rules.

1. A color for the background
2. A color used to frame your papers – same color for the border, if you have one
3. Ink used for the story of your report (black is easy to read).

o   Do not use neon colored display boards or lettering. It takes away from the display and does not look professional. Also, the light in the room causes a glare that reflects off the letters, making them difficult to read.

Look on the next page at an example of a display board. Notice that it is simple, neat, well organized and invites a person to visit and learn more. And isn't that what you want? For the Judges to be attracted like a magnet to your project!

Use your creativity. Envision in your mind how you want your board to look. On a piece of paper sketch a design that is in balance and flows.

Make copies of your sketch. Use crayons or colored pencils to try out different color combinations.

Materials
- For supplies, look at **Shopping List 2**.

- Before attaching anything permanently to the display board, arrange and lay the border (if you have one), titles, sections of your project report, charts and tables, photos, and illustrations in a neat and logical order.

Display Boards
- A display board is made up of sturdy material, has 3 panels that folds out so that the board can stand up by itself. Most schools want you to use the standard size tri-fold display board, which is 36" tall x 48" wide. These boards come pre-made in 1-ply, 2-ply or foam and can be purchased at your local teacher's store, Wal-Mart, Michaels, Joann Fabrics or at Amazon.com (https://amzn.to/3JobiYL). They are inexpensive and can be purchased in different colors.

- We do not recommend making your own display board because it is time consuming and will never look as professional as the store-bought ones.

- On the back of the display board, list your name, school, grade and science teacher's name with a black color Sharpie Permanent Fine Point Marker.

- Use a glue stick or rubber cement to attach your sheets of paper to the display board. Double-sided tape works well for attaching photos.

On the next page is a diagram of how to arrange your display board.

How to Arrange Your Display Board

Arrange the display board like a newspaper, so that the viewer can read from top to bottom, left to right. Include each step of your project in this order: Abstract, Question, Hypothesis, Variables, Background Research, Materials Supply List, Experimental Procedure, Results, Conclusion, Future Directions

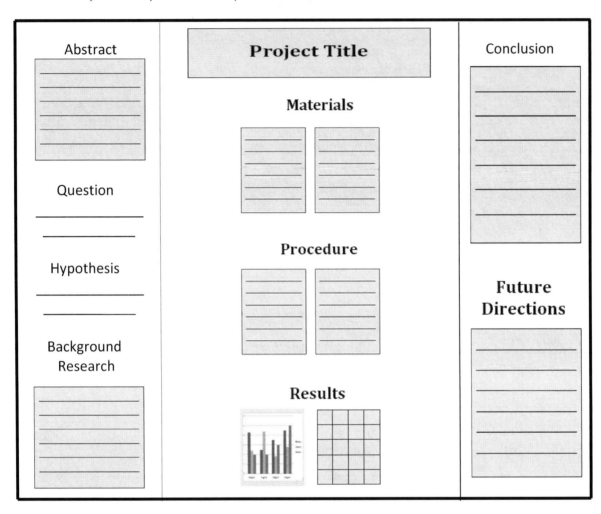

Place these on the table in front of your display board:

Abstract	Project Report	Models Cages Items Studies Surveys	Science Log

Header

Optional: A header sits on top of the display board and inserts into the 1st and 3rd panel. It makes the display board sturdier.

It provides extra space for the Project Title.

It grabs the viewer's attention.

Project Title, Subtitles & Captions

For individual students, title tags, such as Problem, Hypothesis, Data, etc. can be easily made on the computer and printed on card stock at your local printer. Teacher stores also carry these titles.

Project Title

The Project Title is a shortened version of the conclusion in your project paper. Grab the audience's attention by writing an interesting Project Title.

Lettering Sizes on Display Board

o   Make Title letters larger than the subtitles – 150+ pt., at least 2" tall. It needs to be visible from across the room.

119

o Make the headings 32+ pt. It needs to be visible 5 feet away.

o Make the subheadings 20+ pt. or at least 1" tall.

o Make the Captions 12 – 16 pt.

More Tips
o Make the Title Headings look professional. Large repositionable or stencil letters are good alternative to printed text. Look at Shopping List 2 to find out where to purchase these materials.

o You can design the letterheads on a computer. If your home printer does not print sharp looking images, email a pdf file to your local print shop. They can make copies using color cardboard stock.

o Place the title at the top of the middle panel or on a header.

o Use a darker color for the title and subtitles such as dark blue, green, royal blue, medium green and purple.

o Lighter colors can be used such as light blue, yellow, light green as a background for the letters, but it really isn't necessary if you have a white display board.

o Display photographs, illustrations, drawings, charts and tables underneath subheadings.

Pages on Display
o **Fonts**
   ▪ Use a font size of 16 pt. for the text on your display board.

   ▪ Use font style Arial, Times New Roman or Calibri. Do not use more than 2 or 3 different font styles on your board.

   ▪ Use *italics* or bold only for emphasis. Do not use either of them for all the text.

   ▪ Don't use script or artistic fonts because it is too hard to read.

   ▪ Do not place any text on top of a picture because it is difficult to read.

   ▪ Don't use all CAPS because it makes it very hard to read.

   ▪ Do not use white letters with a black or dark background because it is too difficult to read.

- Type and print the report pages that are going to be displayed on the display board. Make the print large enough so that a person standing in front of your table can read it without squinting or leaning forward to see.

o **Border around the report pages**
  - The border needs to be one of the 3 to 5 contrasting colors from your color scheme. This will make your pages stand out, especially if you have a white or light color display board background. Colored construction paper comes in two sizes with many color choices.
    9" x 12" (https://tinyurl.com/y7um9rbm)
    18" x 24" (http://amzn.to/1Qc7WIP)

  - An easy way of creating a border is to put sheets of construction paper behind the white paper containing the sections of your Project Report. Choose a color that matches the title letters. Look at Shopping List 2 to see where to purchase.

  - If you have to buy large sheets of construction paper, cut them to size using a paper cutter because it makes a more professional looking edge. Use a ruler and pencil on the wrong side of the paper. Lightly mark the outer margins where you will cut. Use a paper cutter at school or at your local print shop.

  - Don't put different colors under each section of paper. It will make the board look chaotic.

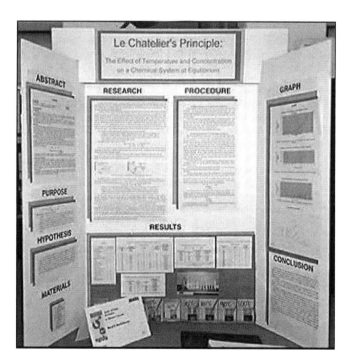

o Computer generated tables, graphs and charts look best. If you draw them by hand, make your drawings neat. Use colored pencils to accent the varying results.

o When possible, have a focal point from which the other pages, tables, graphs, charts and photos stem. This will create continuity and flow. (see next page)

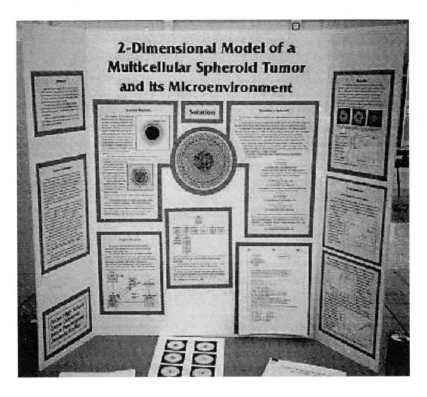

- o Number each graph or image and put them in numerical order.

- o Have a caption under each graph, illustration and photo. Format it to fit the length of the image. Print the caption on white paper. The caption needs to be placed within the colored frame. Look at the following example:

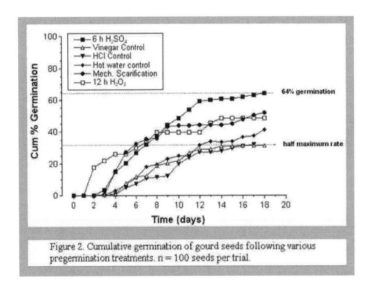

Figure 2. Cumulative germination of gourd seeds following various pregermination treatments. n = 100 seeds per trial.

Border for the Display Board
- o Purchase colored construction paper or repositionable borders at your local office supply store or at Amazon.com (https://tinyurl.com/4snj48eu)

- o Repeat one of the main 3 to 5 contrasting colors from your color scheme. This will create a cohesive design.

- o Because it makes a frame around the display board, it draws the viewer into the space just as a frame around a picture.

- o The border also helps the viewer to concentrate on the board and invites them in to take a closer look.

Notice how the homemade border matches the color scheme. It is quite an eye-catching board with only 4 colors, including the background black board.

- o Attach three-dimensional objects to the display board at the fair - not at home.

- o Look at more examples of display boards in the Appendix of this book.

Pictures
Use photos, diagrams or illustrations to present non-numerical data, models that explain your results, or to show your experimental set-up. Don't put text on top of any of these images.

- o 8" X 10" and 5"x 7" are excellent sizes for your display board. Choose one size for all your photos.
- o Place them in sequential order.

- o Remember to frame them in one of the 3 to 5 colors of your color scheme.

- o Photo stores can enlarge them for you. Some print shops can usually reproduce them for less cost. Make one copy first to check the quality.

- o Follow the KIS principle - Keep it Simple!

Illustrations

- ○ To create poster size images, first draw in pencil and then retrace your drawings and sketches.

- ○ Using an Opaque Projector at school, tape a large piece of paper on the wall and trace the outline of your drawing projection.

- ○ It is important to make the drawings in proportion to the other materials that are on your display board.

Display Placed on the Table Top

Ask your science teacher if you are permitted to cover the table with a cloth. If so, coordinate the color with the color scheme of your display board.

Abstract and Project Report

- ○ Place each sheet of the Abstract and Project Report in individual 3-ring plastic sheet protectors. They can be purchased at your local office supply store look at Shopping List #2.

- ○ Adhering to your color scheme, put the Abstract and Project Report in a 3-ring notebook. Place the Abstract at the front of the notebook.

The Abstract can be either on the display board, in a separate folder on the table, or in the front of the project report folder. Follow the rules of your science fair that you are attending.

- ○ Print a label and place it on the front cover of the notebook. The label must read the title of your project.
- ○ Place the notebook(s) on the table in front of your display board.

Models and Equipment

- ○ Do not allow the models, equipment or parts of the display hang over the table.

- ○ Keep everything off the floor.

- ○ Neatly arrange the model and or equipment in an organized fashion, along with your Abstract & Project Report and Science Log on the table in front of the display board.

- ○ If your project is complicated, you may want to point out certain details. Here are a couple of ideas.

    1. **Companion Board**: Have a small black board that stands on the table that summarizes a process with explanation and images or explains terminology for a lay person.

Elmer's 20" x 30" Foam Board (https://amzn.to/1HkToj5)
Elmer's Project Stand (https://amzn.to/1HkUfAy)
X-ACTO Knife (https://amzn.to/1HkWuUi)

With an X-ACTO knife, cut the board to 12" x 9". Here is a video that shows you how to cut the foam board. (https://tinyurl.com/3hneecwf)

Print your information on white paper with black ink. Here are examples (Science Buddies: 2015)

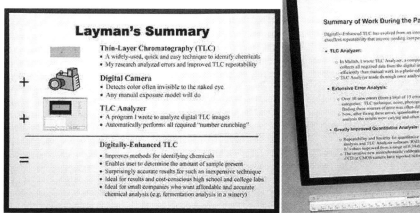 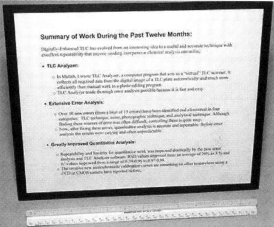

2. If there is room on your large display board, you can have a summary section. Using bullet points and larger header style fonts, you can call attention to significant points. This is a separate section than your abstract.

What Not to Do with Your Display Board
- Don't make the display board so tall that people cannot read what is at the top or stoop down to look at the bottom. Purchase or make a display board that is no taller than 48". Some Big Fairs (sometimes called a Top Fair) may suggest otherwise. Look on the next page.

The board on the right looks good on the floor, but can you image how tall it is going to be when placed on a table at the fair?

o   Don't make a header that casts a shadow on the top of the board. A shadow makes it difficult to read the text and captions.

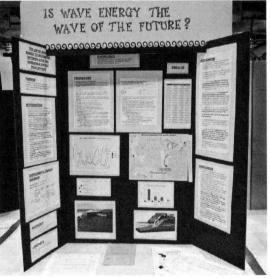

Notice how this header casts a shadow on the left panel. It also interrupts the print on the top left side of that panel.

o Don't make a display board that has side panels that are so deep that the viewer would have to "walk" into the board to view the displays.

Big Fairs / Top Fairs

If you'll be competing at a Big Fair (also called, Top Fairs) sponsored by Intel-ISEF, JSHS, Conrad Foundation Spirit of Innovation, major corporations or larger state and regional fairs, you will probably need to use a display board much larger than the standard 36" x 48" three panel boards that are seen at most science fairs.

Before you create your display, check the rules to see what the maximum display board size is, and be sure the board will fit in the vehicle that will take you to the science fair. If you'll be shipping your display ahead, you'll need to comply with the regulations of the shipping company so that your package arrives undamaged.

Constructing a Modular Display

Participants at big science fairs have another option. They can create their displays using two boards that can be easily transported or shipped and then assembled at the science fair. These are known as modular displays.

The modular display begins with a standard 36" x 48" tri-fold board as the foundation. You can then use another board to create more space for displaying your project:

Look on the next page for suggestions on how to create larger display boards.

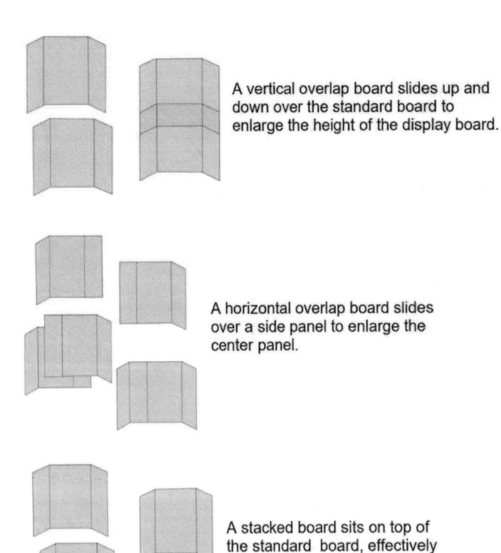

A vertical overlap board slides up and down over the standard board to enlarge the height of the display board.

A horizontal overlap board slides over a side panel to enlarge the center panel.

A stacked board sits on top of the standard board, effectively doubling your display space

You can combine these modular boards in any number of ways to create the exact look you want.

Construction Technique Tips
Trim the edges of the boards with an X-ACTO knife guided by a metal straight edge, such as a ruler or T-square. Because of the thickness of foam core boards, it is wise to make a shallower preliminary cut before the second final cut.

Protect the surface of your desk or table with a piece of heavy cardboard, scrap foam board or cutting mat.

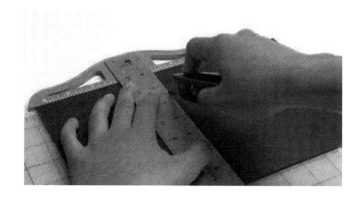

The most secure way of assembling your modular display is to use small nuts and bolts at least ¾" long. Do this by making holes with an awl (a small pointed tool used for piercing holes) or nail.

Another way to connect stacked boards is to use heavy packing tape or duct tape. Remember that when you remove the tape, you'll tear the board. To prevent that from happening, first lay down a strip of tape that will not be removed and attach the tape that will be removed to it.

More Suggestions for Display Boards Used at Top Fairs

o Do a rough sketch of how the components of your display will be put together. That way, when you print out the material for the board, you'll be aware of where the "breaks" between the panels are located.

o Before bringing your display to the science fair, go through a "dry run" assembly so you can work out any glitches ahead of time.

o Check the rules to see if you will need to display an official abstract or provide credits for the images.

o Make sure none of your images are prohibited.

o It's a good idea to number and provide captions for charts, tables and images.

o At a top fair, you will be expected to copy the style of professional journals. Refer to figures in your text, use their respective number.

When Traveling with Your Display Board Long Distances

If you have to travel long distances with your board, then you will want to protect it. Here are some suggestions.

o If traveling by car or plane, you can use a traveling case made by Road Case USA. Make sure to measure your board when it is folded so you know what size to purchase. (https://tinyurl.com/mva4mf56)

o   Moving companies sell picture or mirror boxes.
o   For a fee, moving companies may be willing to crate your display board.

o   Images, photos and illustrations, if large, can be placed in a cardboard tube.

o   Whatever method you use for transporting your board, be sure that you secure 2 types of shipping labels: 1) flat taped on label. 2) luggage label attacked to a strap or handle.

Move on to the next page to see the checklist.

Display Board & Table Display Outcomes Checklist

Print and save the checklist.

Place your display board on a table so you can view it as if it were at the science fair. Then evaluate your display board as you go through each item on the checklist.

My science fair project Display Board includes the following elements...	✓
My display board and materials on the table include: Title Abstract (placed on board, on table in separate folder, and/or in front of Project Report folder) Big Question Variables & Hypothesis Background Research Materials And Supply List Experimental Procedure Data Analysis & Discussion [included data chart(s) and graph(s)] Conclusion Acknowledgements (placed on board and/or written in Project Report) Project Report Bibliography Science Log	
The display board is not more than 48" in height unless going to a Top Fair.	
Side panels aren't so wide that the viewer has to walk into the board to read the back panel.	
I only used 3 – 5 colors on my board including black ink.	
The sections are organized like a newspaper and are easy to follow.	
The Project Title grabs the crowd's attention from across the room.	
The headings are visible to a person walking by my table.	
The fonts used for the text papers are easily read. They are at least 16 pt.	
All charts and tables convey accurate information about the results of my experiment.	
All text, photos, illustrations, charts and graphs have a border around them. They are uniform in size and large enough to see when standing at my table.	
The display board is neat looking and it draws the viewer into the board.	
I proofread the headings and material on the display board.	
I read and followed all the rules for making the display board for my particular science fair.	

Are you all done? Did you finish your display board? Achieve your outcome? If YES – Congratulations! Then print and attach this checklist to your Science Log. Date the entry. Only proceed to the next step after you have completed your display board and table display items.

Whoopie! The Science Fair!

Preparing to Go to the Fair

Eliminating "Crutch" Words

 #11

Crutch words are words that are inserted into sentences as we talk. They give us time to think about what we want to say. After a while they become a habit and we are not aware that we are using them.

At the same time, they are very distracting and make us appear ineffective. Many times, people see you as not knowing what you are talking about.

A bit	Felt/Touch	Seem/Seems/Seemed
Actually	Great	To
Almost	Heard/Hear	Seriously
Appear/Appeared to	Honestly	Shrugged his/Her/Their
As though	Like	Shoulders
Awesome	Literally	Slightly
Basically	Look	So
Beginning to	Nearly	Somehow
Can	Obviously	Super
Certainly	Probably	Totally
Decide	Quite	Very
Definitely	Rather	Virtually
Don't forget	Realize	Watch
Essentially	Really	Well
Fantastic	Right	Wonder
Feel/Felt like	See/Saw	

How to Overcome Using Crutch Words
1. Awareness is the beginning of change.

   Videotape your presentation while you practice talking to the Judge at the Science Fair. Notice what crutch word you use the most. Then give your presentation/conversation to the video camera again and do the following:

2. Stand tall. Carry yourself with confidence.

3. Concentrate on what you are saying. Don't worry about what you are going to say. Live in the moment, the now.

4. If you feel nervous, say the mantra that I taught you:
   I live in my actions, not in my feelings.

5. Better yet, change your language: *I am excited. I am pumped!*
   The language we use changes our experience.

6. Accept that it is going to take time to change old habits. Studies show that it takes 21 days to change a behavior. Even if it takes longer than 21 days, stick with your plan. Eventually you will experience the change you worked so hard to achieve. By doing the above, you will gradually eliminate crutch words.

How-To-Do A Classroom Science Fair Presentation
Rehearse Your Presentation
Time to Wow Your Teachers and Friends
Letter "B" on the Timeline

Sometimes students are asked to do a presentation to their classmates before the actual Science Fair.

I personally extend my congratulations to you for doing such an extraordinary job! You have truly lived the saying, "Being in action creates my success."

You have *reeeally* learned a lot. Believe it or not, it is all in your memory. Did you know that your brain is the most sophisticated computer and digital camera that exist on the planet? Therefore, it is not necessary for you to memorize your presentation. You lived it with every step that you took. So don't concern yourself with knowing the facts.

Just like everything we have discussed so far, attitude is everything. Then comes know-how. Many of the following strategies can be applied when answering the Judge's questions or doing a presentation before your classmates.

Schedule Your Rehearsal Time
You will need to schedule a total of 2 hours, 15-minute increments, for this section so you will feel totally relaxed when you do your presentation or have a discussion with the Judges.

Set the Stage for Your Presentation

Here is my special **SECRET FILES** #12 to help put you at ease.

It is natural to feel a little nervous when giving a presentation. How do you overcome that feeling? Well, the famous entertainer and singer, Bruce Springstein, *The Boss*, calls the feelings in his stomach and throat, and sweaty hands - *EXCITED.*

Yes, change your words and you will change your experience! Did you know that Anthony Robbins, the motivational guru, jumps up and down, claps his hands and says a mantra before going on stage? What are you going to do?

Get *exciiited* about doing your presentation - of course! It's easy. Jump up and down! Shout hurray! When you are excited, the audience is excited and has fun.

Gestures
Be natural and relaxed. Have in your mind that the outcome of this experience is FUN!!! What you are really having is a conversation with a whole bunch of friends.

We naturally use gestures (movement with our hands) when we have a normal conversation without thinking about it. Using natural gestures won't distract from a presentation.

Be aware of the following:
- Keeping your hands out of your pockets
- Handcuffing your hands behind your back
- Keeping your arms crossed in front of your stomach or chest
- Keeping your hands on your hips
- Putting your hands anywhere on your face

Eye Contact
The rule of thumb for eye contact is 1 to 3 seconds per person. Try to focus on one person at a time. After all, these are your friends, your classmates! Don't just look at them, *see them.*

Using Your Voice
Pretend that you are talking to someone in the back of the room. -This is called projecting your voice. *End of Secret Files #12.*

The Presentation
Take time to rehearse, not memorize, your presentation in front of a mirror. Practice on your parents, grandparents, brothers and sisters, the dog. Videotaping yourself during these practices can be helpful.

Ask your "practice audience" to tell you what they especially liked and one thing that could improve your presentation. In this way your presentation will become a natural part of you - like having a conversation with your best friend about a topic that is very familiar to you.

Have you ever heard the saying?
Tell them what you're going to tell them...
Tell them...
Then tell them what you told them!

You may be asking yourself, "How do I do that?"

- **Tell them what you're going to tell them...**
  Develop a clear preview sentence of your main points. Give an introductory remark. This is called a "preframe". It sets the audience's mood before you begin your presentation. Be sure to smile / laugh slightly ... to set the stage.

  Examples:
  - "I would like to tell you about how I started this project, what testing procedure I used, and the results."

  - "Before we begin, I'd like to tell you that I'm excited to tell you about my science project."

  - "Before we begin, I want to warn you, you're really going to have fun learning about my science fair project because it is so extraordinary."

- **Tell them...**
  Talk through each point from your preview sentence.
  - On small note cards put one keyword to remind you of the main points you want to cover during your presentation.

  - Number the cards...1, 2, 3, ... in case they get dropped!

  - During your presentation keep the note cards in your hand or on a table / desk.

- **Tell them what you told them...**
  Review the main points. "I've tried in these past few minutes to give you an overview of how this project started, what testing procedure was used, and the results.

  Conclude your presentation with a strong, positive statement...
  "I learned.... (only one sentence). I would be happy to take any questions at this time."

How to Answer Questions After Your Presentation
- Prepare for questions. Anticipate what questions your audience may have by thinking of questions that you may ask a presenter.

- Repeat the question after someone asks his or her question.

- Maintain your style. Answer your friend's question as if you were having a private conversation.

- Involve the whole audience in your answer. Look at everyone when you answer the question.
- Use your Display Board or Companion Board as a visual aid.

- Ask your teacher a few days before the presentation if s/he has a pointer you can use. If she doesn't, you can always use a ruler. Stand on the side of the board so you do not block your audience's view.

Tips on How to Prepare for the Day of the Science Fair
Prepare for your conversation with the Judges
Notice that I said, "conversation." This is not a presentation. You know what your project is all about because you created it and executed your plan from beginning to end.

Read the section in this book on questions the Judges may ask. Review your Project Report and Abstract. Those two documents will prepare you. Then write out a 1 to 2 sentence summary of what your project is all about. Include:
- how you got the idea for the project – purpose of your project
- how you conducted the experiment
- the results of the experiment and the conclusions you were able to draw

Judges want to know you understand the theory behind the project and why you got the results you did, so be prepared to answer their questions, even if they interrupt you in the middle of the speech. You can point to items on your display board or companion board that illustrate points that you are making.

What Will the Judges Ask You?

o How much help you received from others

o What problems you ran into and how you fixed them

o Three most interesting things you learned when doing your project

o Why this research is important

o What further research you would consider doing

o Reread **How Judges Think** for more possible questions.

Practice explaining your project to a friend or family member. Are you using terms that are understandable to them? Can they understand your graphs and tables? If not, revise your explanation.

Create a list of questions and practice answering them. Videotaping yourself during these practices can be helpful. Eliminate those crutch words!

If any time you feel scared or unsure, just say to yourself, *I live in my actions, not in my emotions*!

Get up – stretch. It's been a great day! I know you have given your all today. Be proud of yourself. You have done an excellent job.

Today You Are Going to the Science Fair!
Letter "A" on Your Timeline

Today is the BIG DAY!
You are prepared.
You are confident.

Here is your 1st Prize ribbon in advance!
You deserve it for all your efforts

Is your science fair one where you'll have the chance to talk with the Judges? If so, consider yourself lucky! When you have the opportunity to explain your project in person, you can create a positive impression with the Judges and increase your chances of placing in the competition.

Some Last Minute Tips

- **Have fun!** That means to enjoy yourself and the experience of the Science Fair. It does not mean to party. What it does mean is to relax and enjoy the "fruits of your labor."

- **You are not your project or display board**. The Judges are evaluating your project, not you. They will be looking at how you present it in written, verbal and graphic form.

- **Practice one more time** what you are going to say to the Judges.

- **Be Professional and Dress Your Best**
  Make a first great impression with the Judges. It *reeealy* makes a difference. Have your image represent the pride and confidence you have in yourself and belief that you did an extraordinary, super, cool science fair project!

  Dress neatly and professionally. Leave the jeans and shorts at home! When you give a professional appearance, the Judges will take you seriously and listen to what you have to say.

- **Bring extra materials with you** in case you have to fix your display the last minute: scissors, tape, glue, letters, paper, table cloth.

  Have you included an extension cord if you need electricity for your project?

  Did you pack your Project Report with Bibliography and Abstract in a 3-ring notebook? Is each Project Report page in a plastic protector sleeve? How about your Science Log?

- **Bring something to keep you quietly busy** while the Judge visits other booths – a puzzle, book, sketchpad, notepad, homework. DO NOT engage in conversation on your cell phone! And no texting!!!!

- After you set up your display, **introduce yourself to the neighbors** on either side of your booth. Act friendly and professional. Ask them about their project. It will help pass the time until the Judge visits you.

- Have someone **take a picture of you** in front of your display with your camera or cell phone. Then put your cell phone on airplane mode.

- **Stay next to your display at all times**. You do not know when the Judges will come to talk with you. You will not get a high score if you are not present to explain what you did. Besides, you do not want curious hands to handle your display.

  If you have to go to the bathroom, tell a teacher so that she can alert the Judges. Come back as quickly as possible.

- **Keep your materials in order on the table** in front of the display.

- **The Judges**

  In the beginning of this book, we discussed the importance of a person's attitude? It is time to show your winning smile again… the one that radiates from within your soul. Exude with positive enthusiasm. Show the Judges that you are interested in your project.

  - Concede that you may be a little nervous. Allow the feeling to flow through your body and drift away. Accept yourself.

  - If you can, stand when the Judges talk with you.

  - **Be confident in your answers**. Positive body language will show your confidence.

    - Hold your head up, straighten your shoulders.

    - Look the Judge directly into his/her eyes.

    - Do not drink, chew gum, eat or slouch.

    - Speak clearly. Do not mumble your words or talk fast. Do not use those distracting crutch words!

    - Concentrate on what you are saying, not what you're going to say.

    - Give a gentle elbow bump and introduce yourself, "Hi, Mr. (name is on their name tag), I am _____. Good to meet you." Then keep quiet and let the Judge tell you what s/he wants to know.

    - Be honest. If you do not know the answer to a question, then tell the Judge the truth. Look the Judge in the eye, and with confidence, say, "I don't know the answer to that question, but I am curious to find out the answer."

    - Tell the Judges how your project is unique, creative or innovative. They love originality.

- **Treat everyone you meet with respect.** They are human being who deserve to be acknowledged in a positive way.

- **Ask the Judges for feedback <u>after</u> the fair is over**. (If they don't have time right then, ask permission to email them.)

  It is great to receive compliments, but constructive criticism is actually more valuable because it will help you make your project even better next time.

  If you are going to submit your science fair project to one or more Top Fairs, the feedback and changes you make may help you to improve your chances of placing at the Fair(s).

Here are a couple of questions you can ask:
1. What can I do next time to improve my project?
2. Do you know someone who could possibly help me expand this project?

Your last Secret File is on the next page...

Last But Not Least...

This is your last **SECRET FILES**

When the day is over, after the judging takes place, find a private place where you can be by yourself. Close your eyes, take a deep breath through your nose and slowly blow the air out through your mouth. Then, ask yourself ...

"What did I learn from this experience?"
Take another deep breath, pause, wait for an answer.
Then write whatever comes to your mind in your Science Log.
Close your eyes again, take a deep, circular breath and ask...

"What would I do differently next time?"
Take another deep breath, pause, wait for an answer.
Then write whatever comes to your mind in your Science Log.
Close your eyes again, take a deep, circular breath and ask...

"What would I do the same next time?"
Take another deep breath, pause, wait for an answer.
Then write whatever comes to your mind in your Science Log.
Close your eyes again, take a deep, circular breath and ask...

"What am I most proud about?"
Take another deep breath, pause, wait for an answer.
Then write whatever comes to your mind in your Science Log.
Close your eyes again, take a deep, circular breath and ask...

"How does that make me feel"?
Take another deep breath, pause, and wait for an answer.
Then write whatever comes to your mind in your Science Log.

Now... put a smile on your face... you know, the one that comes from within and makes you feel warm and fuzzy inside. When you have that special feeling of satisfaction, joy, happiness... whatever you want to call that feeling... literally pat yourself on the back, exuberantly, enthusiastically proclaim out loud,

"Congratulations, I did a greaaat job!"

STUDENT'S APPENDIX

Student Printables

Complete Science Fair Project Checklist Check off the items as you complete them. This will keep you on track.	✓
Printed the table of contents.	
Read the section, Before You Begin.	
Printed all the printables.	
Realistically dated my Timeline.	
Purchased items recommended on Shopping List 1 with parents' permission.	
Keeping a Science Log	
Using a Day-Timer	
Read *What Judges Think* and *Judges Score Sheet* so will know what to do in advance to produce an excellent science fair project.	
Chose a category of science.	
Chose a subcategory.	
Chose a topic.	
Met with my teacher and parent(s). They each approved my topic.	
Read all the information on The Scientific Method.	
Wrote a Big Question.	
Printed and checked off all the items on the Science Fair Project Big Question Outcomes Checklist. Attached the Checklist to my Science Log and dated the entry.	
Met with teacher and parent(s). Got approval to do my background research.	
Background Research ° Completed Keyword Worksheet. ° Completed Question Word Worksheet. ° Found at least 3 to 5 original research references. ° Printed and checked off all the items on the Background Research Outcomes Checklist. ° Evaluated my sources to determine if they were excellent references. ° Wrote notes on note cards. ° Kept track of bibliography on the Bibliography Worksheet. ° Printed and checked off all the items on the Bibliography Outcomes ° Checklist. Attached the Checklist to my Science Log and dated the entry.	
Variables ° Wrote my variables. ° Printed and checked off all the items on the Variables Outcomes Checklist. Attached the Checklist to my Science Log and dated the entry.	
Hypothesis ° Wrote my hypothesis.	

° Printed and checked off all the items on the Hypothesis Outcomes Checklist. Attached the Checklist to my Science Log and dated the entry.	
Filled out Proposal Form.	
Met with my teacher and parent(s). Got approval from both to proceed with project.	
Made a materials and supply list. Purchased / borrowed what I needed.	
Designed my experiment. ° Printed and checked off all the items on the Experimental Procedure Checklist. Attached the Checklist to my Science Log and dated the entry. ° Printed and checked off all the items on the Materials List Outcomes Checklist. Attached the Checklist to my Science Log and dated the entry.	
Project Experiment ° Did my experiment 3 to 5 times (fair test). ° Printed and checked off all the items on the Project Experiment Outcomes Checklist. Attached the Checklist to my Science Log and dated the entry.	
Data ° Created charts and graphs. ° Analyzed my data. ° Drew conclusions. ° Printed and checked off all the items on the Data Analysis, Graph and Drawing Conclusions Outcomes Checklists. Attached the Checklists to my Science Log and dated the entries.	

Wrote my Project Report. Included:
° Title Page
° Table of Contents
° Introduction
° Big Question
° Background Research
° Experimental Procedure
° Materials List
° Data Analysis & Discussion
° Conclusion
° Ideas for Future Research
° Acknowledgements
° Bibliography
° Wrote my Project Report Paper
  • Wrote 1st draft and had someone edit it.
  • Wrote 2nd draft and rechecked it.
  • Wrote final copy and printed on clean white paper either from my home printer or at a print shop.
° Printed and checked off all the items on the Project Report Outcomes Checklist. Attached the Checklist to my Science Log and dated the entry.
 	
Wrote my Abstract. Included:
° Project Title (included my name, school name)
° Purpose of the Project – experiment	

° Hypothesis ° Description of the procedure ° Results ° Conclusions ° Printed and checked off all the items on the Abstract Outcomes Checklist. Attached the Checklist to my Science Log and dated the entry.	
° Constructed an exhibit or display board ° Printed and checked off all the items on the Display Board & Table Display ° Outcomes Checklist. Attached the Checklist to my Science Log and dated the entry.	
° Prepared for and gave a verbal presentation to my class (optional).	
° Prepared my 3–5-minute presentation for the Judge(s)	
Day of the Science Fair ° Dressed neatly and professionally ° Prepared a box with extra materials to fix the display board if necessary. Included all equipment and extension cord (if needed). ° Brought something to keep myself quietly busy at the fair. ° Did the "Last But Not Least" exercise.	

Timeline - Insert dates according to directions following the template below.

AF	**Before You Begin**	
AE	Timeline	
AD	Shopping List 1	
AC	**Science Log**	
AB	Day-Timer	
AA	**The Scientific Method**	
	Topic Research	
Z	**Choose a Category**	
Y	**Determine Subcategory**	
X	**Choose a Topic**	
W	**Teacher & Parent's Approval**	
V	**Big Question**	
U	Proposal Form	
T	**Teacher & Parent's Approval**	
S	Background Research / Bibliography / Note Cards	
R	Keywords & Keyword Questions	
Q	**Determine Variables**	
P	**Write Hypothesis**	
O	**Meet with Your Teacher**	
N	**Write Experimental Procedure**	
M	Materials List	
L	**Teacher & Parent's Approval**	
K	Shopping List 2	
J	**Do Your Experiment**	
I	**Analyze Data & Draw Conclusions** / Analyze Data	
H	**Draw Conclusions**	
G	**Communicating Your Results** / **Write Project Report Paper** / Write 1st Draft	
F	Write 2nd Draft	
E	Write Final Copy	
D	**Write Abstract**	
C	**Design & Create a Display Board**	
B	**Rehearse Presentation**	
A	**Day of Science Fair**	

Start Here →

TIMELINE

Directions on How to Use the Timeline
Start at point A and move left along the horizontal line to point AF.
Write the dates the OUTCOMES are to be completed in the light gray boxes.

Examples:
Input the date of the Science Fair Exhibit in the top gray box of A.
Move to the left to line B, input the date you will do your Presentation.

Continue inserting the dates until you finish writing the date that you are going to start your science fair project.

Science Log Printable

The most difficult thing about keeping a science notebook is remembering to use it at each and every point in your project. With such a detailed account of your project activities, you will be able to go back to a previous step whenever you need to. You will also find it easier to analyze your data and write your Project Report.

Fold this checklist into quarters, using a paper clip, put it in your Day-Timer. At the end of each day, move it to the following day.

What goes into your notebook? Everything...Everyday single day that you work on your project or write an observation about your experiment!

The more details you can include, the better:
o Any form of brainstorming that led you to making a decision.
o Every step you took - one by one.
o What worked and what didn't work.
o What you had to go back and re-do.
o What new insights you achieved.
o What conclusions you drew.

Remember to:
o Write or print legibly.
o Put a date next to each entry.
o Number each page in sequential order.
o Keep the entries in sequential order.
o Do not leave an empty page.
o Place an X in large empty spaces on each page.
o Make entries brief – do not need to use complete sentences.
o Write down any thoughts that come to you about the project.
o Make notes of all test measurements.
o Make a note of anything you need to look up later.
o Staple or tape all loose papers on the day you wrote or printed them.

Things to include:
o Drawings or photographs of your lab setup and results of experiments (you can glue or staple these into your notebook)
o Any math calculations (so you can double check later, if you need to)
o Phone numbers or email addresses of anyone you have contacted about your project

Bibliography Worksheet

| NO. | Source: | ☐ Book | ☐ Magazine | ☐ Newspaper | ☐ Website | ☐ Research Journal | ☐ Other |

Author's Last Name		First Name		Middle Initial
Date Published		Publication/Website Title
Title of Article	
Place Published		Publisher		Editor
(if applicable)		(books only)		(if applicable)
Edition		Volume Number		Page Number(s)
Website is a	☐ Company ☐ Organization ☐ Government ☐ Newspaper/Magazine ☐ Research Journal ☐ Other
Website URL: https://

| NO. | Source: | ☐ Book | ☐ Magazine | ☐ Newspaper | ☐ Website | ☐ Research Journal | ☐ Other |

Author's Last Name		First Name		Middle Initial
Date Published		Publication/Website Title
Title of Article	
Place Published		Publisher		Editor
(if applicable)		(books only)		(if applicable)
Edition		Volume Number		Page Number(s)
Website is a	☐ Company ☐ Organization ☐ Government ☐ Newspaper/Magazine ☐ Research Journal ☐ Other
Website URL: https://

Background Project Research
Keyword Worksheet

Name_____Date_____

Write down your Big Question because it's going to direct you to look for the answer.

_____

_____

List the keywords / phrases in the above sentence plus find more keywords. These keyword phrases will help you to research your topic. Here are free online resources for you to search for your keywords and keyword phrases: Magazines, http://www.encyclopedia.com, http://www.wikipedia.org

List 12 – 20 keyword phrases below:

_____   _____

_____   _____

_____   _____

_____   _____

_____   _____

_____   _____

_____   _____

_____   _____

_____   _____

_____   _____

Using your notes, write one keyword phrase in the top right corner of a note card. Do project research by reading magazines, encyclopedias, journals, etc. and trace the information back to its original source.

Keyword Question Worksheet

Name_____Date_____

Question Word	Possible Questions to Ask Print a set of Worksheets for each keyword or keyword phrase that you research. You may not be able to fill out all the questions for each keyword. You may have some of your own questions you would like to ask.	Relevant ? Write *Yes* or *No* next to each question
Who	Who needs _____? Who discovered _____? Who invented_____? Who_____?	
What	What causes_____ to decrease / increase? What is _____made of? What _____ made from? What are the characteristics of _____? What is the relationship between _____ and _____? What is _____ used for? What is the history of _____? What _____?	
When	When does _____cause _____? When was _____discovered? When_____?	

Where	Where does _____ occur?	
	Where do we use _____?	
Why	Why does _____ happen?	
	Why does _____ happen?	
	Why _____ __?	
How	How is this project unique?	
	How does _____ happen?	
	How does _____ work?	
	How does _____ detect _____?	
	How do you measure _____?	
	How can _____ be used?	
	How _____?	

As you do your research think of the type of formulas or equations you might need to analyze the results of your experiments. Record these in your Science Log.

Staple or tape all the Question Word Worksheets in your Science Log after you complete them.

Variables & Hypothesis Worksheet

Name: _____ Date:_____

Big Question	Independent Variable (What I change)	Dependent Variables (What I observe)	Controlled Variables (What I keep the same)

Write Your Hypothesis
If I do _____
_____
then
_____
_____
this will happen.

Teacher's Approval: _____ Date:_____

Attach to your Science Log.

Proposal Form for Individuals & Teams

Print 3 copies - 1 each for your parent(s), teacher and Science Log. Bring copies to your meeting.

Student(s) Name: Date:

Checklist	✓
The Big Question [I] [we] is/are going to investigate (write your Big Question):	
My Big Question is going to keep me interested for at least a couple of months.	
I will be able to find 3 to 5 original research resources on my topic.	
I will be able to measure changes to the variable using a number that represents a quantity such as count, percentage, length, width, energy, time, voltage, velocity, time. Or, I will be able to measure a variable that is present or not present. Examples: ° Lights On in one trial. Lights Off in another trial. ° Use fertilizer in one trial. Don't use fertilizer in another trial.	
I can design a "fair test" to answer my Big Question.	
I will change only one variable at a time and control the other factors (variables) that might influence my experiment so that they do not interfere with each other.	
My experiment is safe to do. It meets the safety standards outlined by Intel ISEP and my school's rules.	
I have enough time to perform 3 trials of my experiment.	
My experiment meets all the school's science fair rules.	
Check one choice: ° My science fair project requires SRC (Scientific Review Committee) approval. ° My science fair project does not require SRC (Scientific Review Committee) approval.	
I read the List of Science Fair Projects to Avoid and I avoided them.	
I will be able to complete my project before the deadline.	
° I am planning on entering a science fair outside my school. ° My project meets all the science fair requirements. ° I have checked to see what procedure I need to follow to have my project approved for that science fair.	

My parent(s) and I have discussed the above science fair project and I am committed to completing the project on time.

Student's Signature   Date

Continued on nest page.

I have discussed the above science fair project with my child and believe s/he is committed to following through to completion and on time. I agree t o supervise the safety of the project that my child performs at home.

Parent Signature   Date
I approve the Big Question and respective science fair project.

Teacher Signature   Date

This form was adapted from the Kenneth Lafferty Hess Family Charitable Foundation.

201 Science Fair Project Idea Questions

The following questions were developed by a team of 5th grade teachers in Evanston, IL

Animal Studies
- Are animals territorial?
- At what temperature do germs grow best?
- Do ants like cheese or sugar better?
- Do different kinds of caterpillars eat different amounts of food?
- Do mealworms prefer light or dark environments?
- Do mint leaves repel ants?
- Does an earthworm react to light and darkness?
- Does holding a mirror in front of a fish change what a fish does?
- Does surrounding color affect an insect's eating habits?
- How do animals spend the winter?
- How do day-old domestic chicks behave?
- How do different environments affect the regeneration of plant life?
- How do mealworms react to various surfaces?
- How does an earthworm population relate with soil type?
- How far does a snail travel in one minute?
- How much can a caterpillar eat in one day?
- On which surface can a snail move faster – dirt or cement?
- What behaviors does my cat exhibit most frequently?
- What color of birdseed do birds like best?
- What foods do mealworms prefer?
- What types of birds live around me?
- Which travels faster - a snail or a worm?

Comparative Studies
- Do suction cups stick equally well to different surfaces?
- Do watches keep time the same?
- How does omitting an ingredient affect the taste of a cookie?
- How is the rate of melting snow affected by color?
- What factors affect the growth of bread mold?
- What kind of juice cleans pennies best?
- What type of oil has the greatest density?
- Which amount of air space is the best insulator for storm windows?
- Which cheese grows mold the fastest?
- Which lubricants make it most difficult to pick a screwdriver?
- Which materials keep ice cubes from melting for the longest time?
- Which type of sun glass lens blocks the most light?
- Which freezes faster, cold water or hot water?
- Consumer Testing
- Can radiation be used to preserve food?

- Does temperature affect the results of a soft drink challenge?
- What brand of raisin cereal has the most raisins?
- What type of cleaner removes ink stains best?
- Which brand of diaper holds the most water?
- Which brand of disposable diaper absorbs the most liquid?
- Which brand of popcorn pops the fastest?
- Which brand of popcorn pops the most kernels?
- Which brand of soap makes the most suds?
- Which dish soap makes the most bubbles?
- Which engine oil reduces friction the most?
- Which home insulation works the best?
- Which home smoke detector is most sensitive?
- Which house plant fertilizer works best?
- Which laundry detergent works the best?
- Which paper towel is the strongest?
- Which plastic trash bag is the strongest?
- Which self-adhesive floor tile resists wear the most?
- Which videotape maintains the best picture for the greatest amount of use?
- With which type of battery do toys run the longest?

Earth Sciences
- Analysis of lightning strikes
- Are there local rainfall patterns?
- What is global warming?
- What is inside the Earth?
- What is the best air purification method?
- What is the difference between organic fertilizer and chemical fertilizer?
- What makes the seasons?
- Why is ice slippery>
- Why is the sky blue?

Engineering (You cannot use the Scientific Method for the following ideas. You need to follow the Engineering Design Process. [https://tinyurl.com/5fhb3dt7])
- Can I make a real working telegraph?
- Can I make a wind generator?
- Design and make a local weather computer model that is better than what already exists.
- How can airplane seats be made more comfortable?
- How can amusement rides be made safer?
- How can we design standards for every job function in a warehouse to ensure optimal productivity?
- How do airplanes fly?
- How do light bulbs work?
- How do refrigerators work?
- How much weight can a helium balloon lift?

- Is solar energy really practical?
- Is there a backpack that is more economically designed so that my back will not get injured?
- Is there a better way to have arm rests made in the movie so that I don't have to share?
- Is there a more sanitary way to keep toilets in public restrooms clean?
- What can be done so that when one light goes out on a Christmas tree, all the lights go out?
- What can be done to cut down the echo noise in our school cafeteria?
- What processes and systems can we implement in a building to increase productivity and reduce cost?
- What technology solutions can we customize to drive further improvements in our customer's business?
- Why do boats float?
- Why does chewing gum loose it flavor so fast?

Human Studies
- Can people really have ESP?
- Can you tell time without a watch or clock?
- Do boys or girls have a higher resting heart rate?
- Do children's heart rates increase as they get older?
- Do taller people fun faster than shorter people?
- Does anyone in my class, have the same fingerprints?
- Does exercise affect heart rate?
- Does heart rate increase with increasing sound and volume?
- Does noise affect a person's concentration?
- Does the human tongue have definite areas for certain tastes?
- How accurately do people judge temperature?
- How does coffee affect blood pressure?
- How far can a person lean without falling?
- In my class, who has the smallest hands - boys or girls?
- In my class, who has the biggest feet - boys or girls?
- In my class, who is taller – boys or girls?
- Which student in my class has the greatest lung capacity?
- Who do people need eyeglasses?
- Why do I breathe?
- Why do I get sick?

Physical Sciences / Physics
- Can I make paper frogs that jump with static electricity?
- Can I make solid objects float in the air?
- Can magnetism get iron out of clean sand?
- Can same-type balloons withstand the same amount of pressure?
- Can the design of a paper airplane make it fly farther?
- Can things be identified by just their smell?
- Can you tell what something is just by touching it?

- Can you tell where sound comes from when you are blindfolded?
- Can you use a strand of human hair to measure air moisture?
- Do all colors fade at the same rate?
- Do all objects fall to the ground at the same speed?
- Do liquids cool as they evaporate?
- Do sugar crystals grow faster in tap water or distilled water?
- Do wheels reduce frictions?
- Does a ball roll farther on grass or dirt?
- Does a baseball go father with a wood or metal bat?
- Does an ice cube melt faster than air or water?
- Does sound travel best through solids, liquids or gases?
- Does the color of a material affect its absorption of heat?
- Does the shape of a kite affect its flight?
- Does the size of a light bulb affect its energy use?
- Does the viscosity of a liquid affect is boiling point?
- Does the width of a rubber band affect how far it will stretch?
- Does water with salt boil faster than plain water?
- For how long a distance can speech be transmitted through a tube?
- How can you measure the strength of a magnet?
- How does a dry cell generate electricity?
- How far can a water balloon be tossed to someone before it breaks?
- How much salt does it take to float an egg?
- Using a lever, can one student lift another larger student?
- What common liquids are acid, base or neutral?
- What concentration of bleach is required to kill mold?
- What gets warmer faster – sand or soil?
- What holds two boards together better - a nail or a screw?
- What is a rainbow?
- What is the best way to reduce friction?
- What keeps things colder - plastic wrap or aluminum foil?
- What kind of glue holds two boards together better?
- What kind of things do magnets attract?
- What materials provide the best insulations?
- Which liquid has the highest viscosity?
- Which melt conducts heat best?
- Which type of line carries sound waves best?
- Will a rubber band stretch the same distance every time that the same amount of weight is attached to it?

Plant Studies
- Can plants grow from the leaves?
- Can plants grow without soil?
- Do bigger seeds produce bigger plants?
- Do different kinds of apples have the same number of seeds?
- Do different types of soil hold different amounts of water?

- Do living plants give off moisture?
- Do plants grow bigger in soil or water?
- Do roots of a plant always grow downward?
- Does a green plant add oxygen to its environment?
- Does a plant grow bigger if watered with milk or water?
- Does a plant need some darkness to grow?
- Does it matter in which direction seeds are planted?
- Does music effect the growth of plants?
- Does sugar prolong the life of cut flowers?
- Does temperature affect the growth of plants?
- Does the color of light affect plant growth?
- Dose different kinds of apples have the same number of seeds?
- How do plants get diseases?
- How does centrifugal force affect the germination of corn seeds?
- How does light direction affect plant growth?
- How much weight can a growing plant lift?
- Is there a relationship between plants and insects?
- What are the effects of chlorine on plant growth?
- What are the effects of crowding on plant life?
- What causes plant diseases?
- What percentage of corn seeds in a package will germinate?
- What plant foods contain starch?
- Which plants are easiest to grow from stem cuttings?
- Why are leaves green?
- Will adding bleach to the water to its environment?
- Will bananas brown faster on the counter or in the refrigerator?

Water
- Can the sun's energy be used to clean water?
- Can you separate salt from water by freezing?
- Does a bath use less water than a shower?
- Does baking soda lower the temperature of water?
- Does the color of water affect its evaporation?
- Does warm water freeze faster than cool water?
- How long will it take a drop of food dye to color a glass of still water?
- What materials dissolve in water?
- What type of soil filters water best?
- What types of bacteria are found in tap water?
- Which dissolves best in water - salt or baking soda?
- Will water with salt evaporate faster than water without salt?

Science Fair Topics to Avoid

First and foremost – any project in violation of SCVSEFA, ISEF or California Education Rules and Regulations will most likely not be accepted. If you are intending to move on to TOP level fairs, then do not take a chance. Do not do one of the following projects.

1. Strength/absorbency of paper towels (discouraged because seen too often)
2. Most consumer product testing of the "Which is best?" type (OK grades 6-9 only)
3. Astrology projects
4. Maze running (unless there are variables and controls).
5. Any project that boils down to simple preferences.
6. Anything that requires people to recall what they did in the past because data unreliable.
7. Effect of color on taste, memory, emotion, strength, etc.
8. Optical Illusions
9. Acid rain projects (To be considered, thorough research into the composition of acid rain and a scientifically accurate simulation of it would be necessary.)
10. Battery life comparisons (plug in and run-down type)
11. Any project involving the distillation of alcohol. (not permitted because illegal)
12. Pyramid power
13. Color choices of goldfish, etc.
14. Wing, fin shape comparison (OK if mass is taken into consideration)
15. Projects that do not have a measurable endpoint. (Results need to be expressed in units of growth, size, mass, speed, time, volume, frequency, replication rate, chemical product analysis, etc.)
16. Any topic that requires dangerous, hard to find, expensive or illegal materials.
17. Any topic that requires drugging, pain, or injury to a live vertebrate animal
18. Any topic that creates unacceptable risk (physical or psychological) to a human subject.
19. Any topic that involves collection of tissue samples from living humans or vertebrate animals.
20. Graphology or handwriting analysis.

OK With Variables. If you are in middle school and intend to go on to Top Fairs or expand on your project in years to come, I would avoid the following topics.

21. Crystal growth (OK at middle school)
22. Effect of cola, coffee, etc. on teeth (OK at middle school)
23. Effect of music, video games, etc. on blood pressure (OK with 10 people per group)
24. Reaction Times (OK with 10 per group)
25. Planaria worm regeneration (unless project has >10/group)
26. Detergents vs. Stains (OK at middle school).
27. Basic solar collectors or ovens (OK if engineering design variables included)
28. Basic flight testing, e.g., planes, rockets
29. Basic chromatography (OK at middle school)
30. Effect of colored light, music, or talking on plant growth (OK at middle school)

The following projects may meet all requirements but often do not win awards because they are too commonly encountered by judges. With frequently done projects, acceptance may be granted if they have an original twist with exceptional thoroughness and solid scientific method.

1. Comparison of plant growth in different fertilizers
2. Rusting of nails in different pH solutions.
3. Comparison of strength in different bridge designs.
4. Volcanoes that erupt.

Reasons to Avoid a Topic

o   If the experiments don't involve numerical measurement such as a survey.

o   Consumer products – the science the behind why these products work is at graduate school level. For your experiment to have validity, you would need to have that scientific expertise.

o   Data tends to be unreliable when people give a subjective response.

o   When many students in the past have done a project on this subject.

o   When an experiment is difficult to measure. Example: Effects of light, music or talking to a plant.

o   If the results are obvious (a person's pulse when running) or difficult to measure (effect of music on a person's pulse).

o   Questionable or no scientific validity. Example: handwriting analysis or astrology.

o   When the rules of the science fair are violated.

Powerful Words

Powerful words are excellent influencers. At the same time, don't get so caught up in thinking that you must use and loose track of your goal – to design a display board that represents you and your experience and to feel at ease when presenting to your class or the Judges.

The 5 most persuasive words in the English language
- You
- Free
- Because
- Instantly
- New

The research behind these words has shown over and over that they work.
(https://tinyurl.com/5pdz77yr)

Where to try these words: Calls-to-action, headlines, email subject lines, headings, opening sentences and paragraphs

The 20 most influential words, **via David Ogilvy** (advertising guru)

Amazing	Easy	Miracle	Revolutionary
Announcing	Hurry	Now	Sensational
Bargain	Improvement	Offer	Startling
Challenge	Introducing	Quick	Suddenly
Compare	Magic	Remarkable	Wanted

Where to try these: Headlines, bullet points, subject lines

10 cause-and-effect words and phrases

Accordingly	Consequently	Therefore
As a result	Due to	Thus
Because	For this reason	
Caused by	Since	

Author Darlene Price, the originator of this cause-and-effect list, states what makes these phrases so useful: "Cause-and-effect words make your claims sound objective and rational rather than biased and subjective."

Where to try these: Closing paragraphs, transitions

The Big 5 Hypnotic Power Words

There are dozens of power words you can use, so let's start with what we'll call the Big 5. They trance the brain and cause the person who is listening to believe whatever is written or said immediately after the word is used.

1. Because

   Example: "You're listening to me, you can relax, and because you're relaxing, you can feel comfortable because comfort builds more relaxation, so you can relax even more comfortably and because you're relaxing right now, you can feel more comfort developing inside you."

2. And

   Example: "You can relax and feel comfortable, and the comfort you feel will make you relax even more, and the more you feel the comfort, the more you'll relax. And as you relax, you'll feel more comfortable. As you feel more comfortable, you'll relax more and more. Relaxing more and feeling comfort is important for relaxation, so as you relax and feel comfort and relax even more and feel even more comfort."

3. As

   Example: "As you listen to my voice, you can start to focus your attention inside. As your attention focuses inward, so your unconscious mind begins to take you into trance. As you breathe in and out, you will notice an ever-deepening comfort starting to develop."

4. Imagine

   Example: "Can you imagine going into trance? Imagine yourself drifting on a calm and beautiful river. Picture your muscles becoming loose and limp. See yourself feeling completely relaxed. Then imagine enjoying the most exquisite trance experience."

5. Which Means

   Example: "You have been studying these language patterns for some time now, which means that you are learning something of tremendous value. The fact that you are reading this right now means that you are learning at the unconscious level...."

Each of these power words serves its own purpose, but their power is increased when they're combined.

Example of Judges Score Sheet

Project #: _____ Project Title: _____

Write the project number and the title of the project in the spaces above. Score each of the projects assigned to you in the category that you are judging. Different judges will be assigned different categories, so it is only necessary for you to score your assigned category. Circle the number that best equates to the quality of the project.

PROJECT OBJECTIVES

Originality of investigation   Not Present   Excellent
                                        0   1   2   3   4   5

Clearly stated/answerable question   Not Present   Excellent
                                      0   1   2   3   4   5
Hypothesis phrased as a testable idea with a rationale
                                     Not Present   Excellent

                                     0   1   2   3   4   5

                                                      Score _____/15

PROJECT IMPLEMENTATION

Experiment addresses question and is clearly explained
                                     Not Present   Excellent
                                        0   1   2   3   4

Independent research and experimentation
                                     Not Present   Excellent
                                        0   1   2   3   4
Experimental procedures explained thoroughly so the methods are repeatable by others
                                     Not Present   Excellent
                                        0   1   2   3   4
Clearly defined variables and controls
                                     Not Present   Excellent
                                        0   1   2   3   4
Measurable results
                                     Not Present   Excellent
                                        0   1   2   3   4

                                                      Score _____/20

DATA COLLECTION AND PRESENTATION
Evidence of multiple trials

	Not Present				Excellent
	0	1	2	3	4

Complete data set and summary data are presented

	Not Present				Excellent
	0	1	2	3	4

Data presentation includes tabular, graphic, and written forms

	Not Present				Excellent
	0	1	2	3	4

Data presentation includes discussion of variability of results

	Not Present				Excellent
	0	1	2	3	4

Score _____ /16

DATA INTERPRETATION
Use of appropriate data types and graphics

	Not Present					Excellent
	0	1	2	3	4	5

Data are used to draw a well-supported conclusion

	Not Present					Excellent
	0	1	2	3	4	5

Background information is used to help interpret data

	Not Present					Excellent
	0	1	2	3	4	5

Conclusion includes reflection of possible effects of methods on results

	Not Present					Excellent
	0	1	2	3	4	5

Score _____ /20

PROJECT PRESENTATION
Creativity of presentation

	Not Present				Excellent
	0	1	2	3	4

Clear and thorough explanation of investigation

	Not Present				Excellent
	0	1	2	3	4

Neat and organized presentation of information

	Not Present				Excellent
	0	1	2	3	4

Score _____ /12

RELATED STUDY REPORT

Clearly written in student's own words

	Not Present			Excellent
	0	1	2	3

Clearly relates to science fair project

	Not Present			Excellent
	0	1	2	3

References are properly cited

	Not Present			Excellent
	0	1	2	3

Score _____/9

INTERVIEW

Student is present   Not Present   Excellent
                                        0   4

Student conveys understanding of concepts related to project

	Not Present			Excellent	
	0	1	2	3	4

Score _____/8

TOTAL SCORE   _____/100

Questions Asked at the San Diego Science & Engineering Science Fair

- How did you decide to do this particular project?

- Is this project an expansion of one you did before? If so, what did you add or change?

- How does this science fair project apply to real life?

- How did you determine your sample size?

- Did you choose any statistical test? If so, how did you determine which one to use?

- Will you explain your graph / chart / photos me to?

- Please explain your procedure.

- What do your results mean? How can they apply to everyday life?

- How many times did you repeat your experiment? Test your device or program?

- How is this project different from others that you researched?

- What was the most interesting background reading that you did?

- Where did you get your science supplies?

- What new skills, if any, did you learn by doing this science fair project?

- What is the most important thing you learned by doing this project?

- What changes would you make if you continued this project?

Intel ISEF Categories & Subcategories

The categories of science listed below are those used by Intel ISEF.

Your local, regional, state and country fairs **may or may not** choose to use these categories. Check with the Fair you are participating in for the category listings that are at your level of competition.

Animal Sciences (Code: ANIM)
This category includes all aspects of animals and animal life, animal life cycles, and animal interactions with one another or with their environment.

Examples of investigations included in this category would involve the study of the structure, physiology, development, and classification of animals, animal ecology, animal husbandry, entomology, ichthyology, ornithology, and herpetology, as well as the study of animals at the cellular and molecular level which would include cytology, histology, and cellular physiology.

Subcategories of Animal Sciences:
Animal Behavior (BEH): The study of animal activities which includes investigating animal interactions within and between species or an animal's response to environmental factors. Examples are animal communication, learning, and intelligence, rhythmic functions, sensory preferences, pheromones, and environmental effects on behaviors, both naturally and experimentally induced.

Cellular Studies (CEL): The study of animal cells involving the use of microscopy to study cell structure and studies investigating activity within cells such as enzyme pathways, cellular biochemistry, and synthesis pathways for DNA, RNA, and protein.

Development (DEV): The study of an organism from the time of fertilization through birth or hatching and into later life. This includes cellular and molecular aspects of fertilization, development, regeneration, and environmental effects on development.

Ecology (ECO): The study of interactions and behavioral relationships among animals, and animals and plants, with their environment and with one another.

Genetics (GEN): The study of species and population genetics at the organismal or cellular level.

Nutrition and Growth (NTR): The study of natural, artificial, or maternal nutrients on animal growth, development, and reproduction including the use and effects of biological and chemical control agents to control reproduction and population numbers.

Physiology (PHY): The study of one of the 11 animal systems. This includes structural and functional studies, system mechanics, and the effect of environmental factors or natural variations on the structure or function of a system. Similar studies conducted specifically at the cellular level should select the cellular studies subcategory.

Systematics and Evolution (SYS): The study of animal classification and phylogenetic methods including the evolutionary relationships between species and populations. This includes morphological, biochemical, genetic, and modeled systems to describe the relationship of animals to one another.

Other (OTH): Studies that cannot be assigned to one of the above subcategories.

Behavioral and Social Sciences (Code: BEHA)
The science or study of the thought processes and behavior of humans and other animals in their interactions with the environment studied through observational and experimental methods.

Subcategories:
Clinical and Developmental Psychology (CLN): The study and treatment of emotional or behavioral disorders. Developmental psychology is concerned with the study of progressive behavioral changes in an individual from birth until death.

Cognitive Psychology (COG): The study of cognition, the mental processes that underlie behavior, including thinking, deciding, reasoning, and to some extent motivation and emotion. Neuro-psychology studies the relationship between the nervous system, especially the brain, and cerebral or mental functions such as language, memory, and perception.

Physiological Psychology (PHY): The study of the biological and physiological basis of behavior.

Sociology and Social Psychology (SOC): The study of human social behavior, especially the study of the origins, organization, institutions, and development of human society. Sociology is concerned with all group activities-economic, social, political, and religious.

Other (OTH): Studies that cannot be assigned to one of the above subcategories.

Biochemistry (Code: BCHM)
The study of the chemical basis of processes occurring in living organisms, including the processes by which these substances enter into, or are formed in, the organisms and react with each other and the environment.

Subcategories:
Analytical Biochemistry (ANB): The study of the separation, identification, and quantification of chemical components relevant to living organisms.

General Biochemistry (GNR): The study of chemical processes, including interactions and reactions, relevant to living organisms.

Medicinal Biochemistry (MED): The study of biochemical processes within the human body, with special reference to health and disease.

Structural Biochemistry (STR): The study of the structure and or function of biological molecules.

Other (OTH): Studies that cannot be assigned to one of the above subcategories.

Biomedical and Health Sciences (Code: BMED)
This category focuses on studies specifically designed to address issues of human health and disease.

It includes studies on the diagnosis, treatment, prevention or epidemiology of disease and other damage to the human body or mental systems. Includes studies of normal functioning and may investigate internal as well as external factors such as feedback mechanisms, stress or environmental impact on human health and disease.

Subcategories of Biomedical and Health Sciences:
Disease Diagnosis (DIS): The systematic examination, identification, and determination of disorders and disease through examination at the whole body or cellular levels.

Disease Treatment (TRE): The use of pharmaceuticals and other therapies, including natural and holistic remedies, intended to improve symptoms and treat or cure disorders or disease.

Drug Development and Testing (DRU): The study and testing of new chemical therapies intended to improve symptoms and treat or cure disorders and disease. This testing could include any platform from tissue culture to preclinical animal models. This will include establishing a drug's safety profile and ensuring regulatory compliance.

Epidemiology (EPI): The study of disease frequency and distribution, and risk factors and socioeconomic determinants of health within populations. Epidemiologic investigations may include gathering information to confirm existence of disease outbreaks, developing case definitions and analyzing epidemic data, establishing disease surveillance, and implementing methods of disease prevention and control.

Nutrition (NTR): The study of food, nutrients and dietary need in humans, and the effects of food and nourishment on the body. These studies may include the effects of natural or supplemental nutrients and nutrition.

Physiology and Pathology (PHY): The science of the mechanical, physical, and biochemical functions of normal human tissues, organs, and body systems; and the study of disease-related tissue and organ dysfunction. Pathophysiology is the study of the conditions leading up to a diseased state and includes an investigation of the disturbance responsible for causing the disease.

Other (OTH): Studies that cannot be assigned to one of the above subcategories.

Cellular and Molecular Biology (Code: CELL)
This is an interdisciplinary field that studies the structure, function, intracellular pathways, and formation of cells. Studies involve understanding life and cellular processes specifically at the molecular level.

Subcategories:
Cell Physiology (PHY): The study of the cell cycle, cell function, and interactions between cells or between cells and their environment.

Genetics (GEN): The study of molecular genetics focusing on the structure and function of genes at a molecular level.

Immunology (IMM): The study of the structure and function of the immune system at the cellular level. This includes investigations of innate and acquired (adaptive) immunity, the cellular communication pathways involved in immunity, cellular recognition, graft vs host and host vs graft disease, and interactions between antigens and antibodies.

Molecular Biology (MOL): The study of biology at the molecular level. Chiefly concerns itself with understanding the interactions between the various systems of a cell, including the interrelationships of DNA, RNA and protein synthesis and learning how these interactions are regulated, such as during transcription and translation, the significance of introns and exons or coding issues.

Neurobiology (NEU): The study of the structure and function of the nervous system at the cellular or molecular level.

OTH Other (OTH): Studies that cannot be assigned to one of the above subcategories.

Chemistry (Code: CHEM)
Studies exploring the science of the composition, structure, properties, and reactions of matter not involving biochemical systems.

Subcategories:
Analytical Chemistry (ANC): The study of the separation, identification, and quantification of the chemical components of materials.

Computational Chemistry (COM): A study that applies the discipline and techniques of computer science and mathematics to solve large and complex problems in Chemistry.
Environmental Chemistry (ENV): The study of chemical species in the natural environment, including the effects of human activities, such as the design of products and processes that reduce or eliminate the use or generation of hazardous substances.

Inorganic Chemistry (INO): The study of the properties and reactions of inorganic and organometallic compounds.

Materials Chemistry (MAT): The chemical study of the design, synthesis and properties of substances, including condensed phases (solids, liquids, polymers) and interfaces, with a useful or potentially useful function, such as catalysis or solar energy.

ORG Organic Chemistry (ORG): The study of carbon-containing compounds, including hydrocarbons and their derivatives.

Physical Chemistry (PHC): The study of the fundamental physical basis of chemical systems and processes, including chemical kinetics, chemical thermodynamics, electrochemistry, photochemistry, spectroscopy, statistical mechanics and astro-chemistry.

Other (OTH): Studies that cannot be assigned to one of the above subcategories.

Computational Biology and Bioinformatics (Code: CBIO)
Studies that primarily focus on the discipline and techniques of computer science and mathematics as they relate to biological systems

Studies that include the development and application of data-analytical and theoretical methods, mathematical modeling and computational simulation techniques to the study of biological, behavior, and social systems.

Subcategories of Computational Biology and Bioinformatics:
Biomedical Engineering (BME): The application of engineering principles and design concepts to medicine and biology for healthcare purposes.

Computational Biomodelling (MOD): Studies that involve computer simulations of biological systems most commonly with a goal of understanding how cells or organism develop, work collectively and survive.

Computational Evolutionary Biology (EVO): A study that applies the discipline and techniques of computer science and mathematics to explore the processes of change in populations of organisms, especially taxonomy, paleontology, ethology, population genetics and ecology.

Computational Neuroscience (NEU): A study that applies the discipline and techniques of computer science and mathematics to understand brain function in terms of the information processing properties of the structures that make up the nervous system.

Computational Pharmacology (PHA): A study that applies the discipline and techniques of computer science and mathematics to predict and analyze the responses to drugs.

Genomics **(GEN)**: The study of the function and structure of genomes using recombinant DNA, sequencing, and bioinformatics.

Other (OTH): Studies that cannot be assigned to one of the above subcategories.

Earth and Environmental Sciences (Code: EAEV)

Studies of the environment and its effect on organisms/systems, including investigations of biological processes such as growth and life span, as well as studies of Earth systems and their evolution.

Subcategories:

Atmospheric Science (AIR): Studies of the earth's atmosphere, including air quality and pollution and the processes and effects of the atmosphere on other Earth systems as well as meteorological investigations.

Climate Science (CLI): Studies of Earth's climate, particularly evidential study of climate change.

Environmental Effects on Ecosystems (ECS): Studies of the impact of environmental changes (natural or as a result of human interaction) on ecosystems, including empirical pollution studies.

Geosciences (GES): Studies of Earth's land processes, including mineralogy, plate tectonics, volcanism, and sedimentology.

Water Science **(WAT)**: Studies of Earth's water systems, including water resources, movement, distribution, and water quality.

Other (OTH): Studies that cannot be assigned to one of the above subcategories.

Embedded Systems (Code: EBED)

Studies involving electrical systems in which information is conveyed via signals and waveforms for purposes of enhancing communications, control and/or sensing.

Subcategories:

Circuits (CIR): The study, analysis, and design of electronic circuits and their components, including testing.

Internet of Things **(IOT)**: The study of the interconnection of unique computing devices with the existing infrastructure of the Internet and the cloud.

Microcontrollers **(MIC)**: The study and engineering of microcontrollers and their use to control other devices.

Networking and Data Communication (NET): The study of systems that transmit any combination of voice, video, and/or data among users.

Optics **(OPT)**: The use of visible or infrared light instead of signals sent over wires. The study and development of optical devices and systems devoted to practical applications such as computation.

Sensors **(SEN)**: The study and design of devices that transmit an electrical response to an external device.

Signal Processing **(SIG)**: The extraction of signals from noise and their conversion into a representation for modeling and analysis.

Other (OTH): Studies that cannot be assigned to one of the above subcategories.

Energy: Chemical (Code: EGCH)
Studies involving biological and chemical processes of renewable energy sources, clean transport, and alternative fuels.

Subcategories:
Alternative Fuels (ALT): Any method of powering an engine that does not involve petroleum (oil). Some alternative fuels are electricity, methane, hydrogen, natural gas, and wood.

Computational Energy Science (COM): A study that applies the discipline and techniques of computer science and mathematics to solve large and complex problems in Energy Science.

Fossil Fuel Energy (FOS): Studies involving energy from a hydrocarbon deposit, such as petroleum, coal, or natural gas, derived from living matter of a previous geologic time and used for fuel.

Fuel Cells and Battery Development (FUE): The study, analysis and development of fuel cells and batteries that convert and/or store chemical energy into electricity.

Microbial Fuel Cells (MIC): The study of fuel cells that use or mimic bacterial interactions found in nature to produce electricity.

Solar Materials (SOL): The study of materials used to convert and store solar energy through chemical changes. This includes topics such as thermal storage and photovoltaic materials.

Other (OTH): Studies that cannot be assigned to one of the above subcategories.

Energy: Physical (Code: EGPH)
Studies of renewable energy structures/processes including energy production and efficiency.

Subcategories:
Hydro Power (HYD): The application of engineering principles and design concepts to capture energy from falling and running water to be converted to another form of energy.

Nuclear Power (NUC): The application of engineering principles and design concepts to capture nuclear energy to be converted to another form of energy.

Solar (SOL): The application of engineering principles and design concepts to capture energy from the sun to be converted to another form of energy.

Sustainable Design (SUS): The application of engineering principles and design concepts to plan and/or construct buildings and infrastructure that minimize environmental impact.

Thermal Power (THR): The application of engineering principles and design concepts to capture energy from the Earth's crust to be converted to another form of energy.

Wind (WIN): The application of engineering principles and design concepts to capture energy from the wind to be converted to another form of energy.

Other (OTH): Studies that cannot be assigned to one of the above subcategories.

Engineering: Mechanics (Code: ENMC)
Studies that focus on the science and engineering that involve movement or structure. The movement can be by the apparatus or the movement can affect the apparatus.

Subcategories:
Aerospace and Aeronautical Engineering (AER): Studies involving the design of aircraft and space vehicles and the direction of the technical phases of their manufacture and operation.

Civil Engineering (CIV): Studies that involve the planning, designing, construction, and maintenance of structures and public works, such as bridges or dams, roads, water supply, sewer, flood control and, traffic.

Computational Mechanics (COM): A study that applies the discipline and techniques of computer science and mathematics to solve large and complex problems in Engineering Mechanics.

Control Theory (CON): The study of dynamical systems, including controllers, systems, and sensors that are influenced by inputs.

Ground Vehicle Systems (VEH): The design of ground vehicles and the direction of the technical phases of their manufacture and operation.

Industrial Engineering-Processing (IND): Studies of efficient production of industrial goods as affected by elements such as plant and procedural design, the management of materials and energy, and the integration of workers within the overall system. The industrial engineer designs methods, not machinery.

Mechanical Engineering (MEC): Studies that involve the generation and application of heat and mechanical power and the design, production, and use of machines and tools.

Naval Systems (NAV): Studies of the design of ships and the direction of the technical phases of their manufacture and operation.

Other (OTH): Studies that cannot be assigned to one of the above subcategories.

Environmental Engineering (Code: ENEV)
Studies that engineer or development processes and infrastructure to solve environmental problems in the supply of water, the disposal of waste, or the control of pollution.

Subcategories:
Bioremediation (BIR): The use of biological agents, such as bacteria or plants, to remove or neutralize contaminants. This includes phytoremediation, constructed wetlands for wastewater treatment, biodegradation, etc.

Land Reclamation (ENG): The application of engineering principles and design techniques to restore land to a more productive use or its previous undisturbed state.

Pollution Control (PLL): The application of engineering principles and design techniques to remove pollution from air, soil, and/or water.

Recycling and Waste Management (REC): The extraction and reuse of useful substances from discarded items, garbage, or waste. The process of managing, and disposing of, wastes and hazardous substances through methodologies such as landfills, sewage treatment, composting, waste reduction, etc.

Water Resources Management **(WAT)**: The application of engineering principles and design techniques to improve the distribution and management of water resources.

Other (OTH): Studies that cannot be assigned to one of the above subcategories.

Materials Science (Code: MATS)
The study of the characteristics and uses of various materials with improvements to their design which may add to their advanced engineering performance.

Subcategories:
Biomaterials (BIM): Studies involving any matter, surface, or construct that interacts with biological systems. Such materials are often used and/or adapted for a medical application, and thus comprise whole or part of a living structure or biomedical device which performs, augments, or replaces a natural function.

Ceramic and Glasses (CER): Studies involving materials composed of ceramic and glass – often defined as all solid materials except metals and their alloys that are made by the high-temperature processing of inorganic raw materials.

Composite Materials (CMP): Studies involving materials composed of two or more different materials combined together to create a superior and unique material.

COM Computation and Theory (COM): Studies that involve the theory and modeling of materials.

Electronic, Optical and Magnetic Materials (ELE): The study and development of materials used to form highly complex systems, such as integrated electronic circuits, optoelectronic devices, and magnetic and optical mass storage media. The various materials, with precisely controlled properties, perform numerous functions, including the acquisition, processing, transmission, storage, and display of information.

Nanomaterials (NAN): The study and development of nanoscale materials; materials with structural features (particle size or grain size, for example) of at least one dimension in the range 1-100 nm.

Polymers (POL): The study and development of polymers; materials that have a molecular structure consisting chiefly or entirely of a large number of similar units bonded together, e.g., many synthetic organic materials used as plastics and resins.
Other (OTH): Studies that cannot be assigned to one of the above subcategories.

Mathematics (Code: MATH)
The study of the measurement, properties, and relationships of quantities and sets, using numbers and symbols. The deductive study of numbers, geometry, and various abstract constructs, or structures.

Subcategories:
Algebra (ALB): The study of algebraic operations and/or relations and the structures which arise from them. An example is given by (systems of) equations which involve polynomial functions of one or more variables.

Analysis (ANL): The study of infinitesimal processes in mathematics, typically involving the concept of a limit. This begins with differential and integral calculus, for functions of one or several variables, and includes differential equations.

Combinatorics, Graph Theory and Game Theory (CGG): The study of combinatorial structures in mathematics, such as finite sets, graphs, and games, often with a view toward classification and/or enumeration.

Geometry and Topology (GEO): The study of the shape, size, and other properties of figures and spaces. Includes such subjects as Euclidean geometry, non-Euclidean geometries (spherical, hyperbolic, Riemannian, Lorentzian), and knot theory (classification of knots in 3-space).

Number Theory (NUM): The study of the arithmetic properties of integers and related topics such as cryptography.

Probability and Statistics (PRO): Mathematical study of random phenomena and the study of statistical tools used to analyze and interpret data.

Other (OTH): Studies that cannot be assigned to one of the above subcategories.

Microbiology (Code: MCRO)
The study of micro-organisms, including bacteria, viruses, fungi, prokaryotes, and simple eukaryotes as well as antimicrobial and antibiotic substances

Subcategories:
Antimicrobials and Antibiotics (ANT): The study of a substance that kills or inhibits the growth of a microorganisms.

Applied Microbiology (APL): The study of microorganisms having potential applications in human, animal or plant health or the use of microorganisms in the production of energy.

Bacteriology (BAC): The study of bacteria and bacterial diseases and the microorganisms responsible for causing a disease.

Environmental Microbiology (ENV): The study of the structure, function, diversity and relationship of microorganisms with respect to their environment. This includes the study of biofilms.

Microbial Genetics (GEN): The study of how microbial genes are organized and regulated and their involvement in cellular function.
Virology (VIR): The study of viruses and viral diseases.

Other (OTH): Studies that cannot be assigned to one of the above subcategories.

Physics and Astronomy (Code: PHYS)
Physics is the science of matter and energy and of interactions between the two. Astronomy is the study of anything in the universe beyond the Earth.

Subcategories:
Atomic, Molecular, and Optical Physics (AMO): The study of atoms, simple molecules, electrons and light, and their interactions.

Astronomy and Cosmology (AST): The study of space, the universe as a whole, including its origins and evolution, the physical properties of objects in space and computational astronomy.

Biological Physics (BIP): The study of the physics of biological processes.

Computational Physics (COM): A study that applies the discipline and techniques of computer science and mathematics to solve large and complex problems in Physics and Astrophysics.

Condensed Matter and Materials (MAT): The study of the properties of solids and liquids. Topics such as superconductivity, semi-conductors, complex fluids, and thin films are studied.

Instrumentation (INS): Instrumentation is the process of developing means of precise measurement of various variables such as flow and pressure while maintaining control of the variables at desired levels of safety and economy.

Magnetics, Electromagnetics and Plasmas (MAG): The study of electrical and magnetic fields and of matter in the plasma phase and their effects on materials in the solid, liquid or gaseous states.

Mechanics (MEC): Classical physics and mechanics, including the macroscopic study of forces, vibrations and flows; on solid, liquid and gaseous materials.

Nuclear and Particle Physics (NUC): The study of the physical properties of the atomic nucleus and of fundamental particles and the forces of their interaction.

Optics, Lasers, Masers (OPT): The study of the physical properties of light, lasers and masers.

Quantum Computation (QUA): The study of the laws of quantum mechanics to process information. This includes studies involving the physics of information processing, quantum logic, quantum algorithms, quantum error correction, and quantum communication.

Theoretical Physics (THE): The study of nature, phenomena and the laws of physics employing mathematical models and abstractions rather than experimental processes.

Other (OTH): Studies that cannot be assigned to one of the above subcategories.

Plant Sciences (Code: PLNT)
Studies of plants and how they live, including structure, physiology, development, and classification.

Subcategories:
Agronomy (AGR): Application of the various soil and plant sciences to soil management and agricultural and horticultural crop production. Includes biological and chemical controls of pests, hydroponics, fertilizers and supplements.

Growth and Development (DEV): The study of a plant from earliest stages through germination and into later life. This includes cellular and molecular aspects of development and environmental effects, natural or manmade, on development and growth.

Ecology (ECO): The study of interactions and relationships among plants, and plants and animals, with their environment.

Genetics/Breeding (GEN): The study of organismic and population genetics of plants. The application of plant genetics and biotechnology to crop improvement. This includes genetically modified crops.

Pathology (PAT): The study of plant disease states, and their causes, processes, and consequences. This includes effects of parasites or disease-causing microbes.

Physiology (PHY): The study of functions in plants and plant cells. This includes cellular mechanisms such as photosynthesis and transpiration, and how plant processes are affected by environmental factors or natural variations.

Systematics and Evolution (SYS): The study of classification of organisms and their evolutionary relationships. This includes morphological, biochemical, genetic, and modeled systems.

Other (OTH): Studies that cannot be assigned to one of the above subcategories.

Robotics and Intelligent Machines (Code: ROBO)
Studies in which the use of machine intelligence is paramount to reducing the reliance on human intervention

Subcategories:
Biomechanics (BIE): Studies and apparatus which mimic the role of mechanics in biological systems.

Cognitive Systems (COG): Studies/apparatus that operate similarly to the ways humans think and process information. Systems that provide for increased interaction of people and machines to more naturally extend and magnify human expertise, activity, and cognition.

Control Theory (CON): Studies that explore the behavior of dynamical systems with inputs, and how their behavior is modified by feedback. This includes new theoretical results and the applications of new and established control methods, system modeling, identification and simulation, the analysis and design of control systems (including computer-aided design), and practical implementation.

Robot Kinematics (KIN): The study of movement in robotic systems.

Machine Learning (MAC): Construction and/or study of algorithms that can learn from data.

Other (OTH): Studies that cannot be assigned to one of the above subcategories.

Systems Software (Code: SOFT)
The study or development of software, information processes or methodologies to demonstrate, analyze, or control a process/solution

Subcategories:
Algorithms (ALG): The study or creation of algorithms - step-by-step procedure of calculations
to complete a specific task in data processing, automated reasoning and computing.

Cybersecurity (CYB): Studies involving the protection of a computer or computer system against unauthorized access or attacks. This can include studies involving hardware, network, software, host or multimedia security.

Databases (DAT): Studies that create or analyze data organization for ease of access, management and update.

Operating Systems (SYS): The study of system software responsible for the direct control and management of hardware and basic system operations of a computer or mobile device.

Programming Languages (PRG): Studies that involve the development or analysis of the artificial languages used to write instructions that can be translated into machine language and then executed by a computer.

Other (OTH): Studies that cannot be assigned to one of the above subcategories.

Examples & Critiques of Science Fair Boards

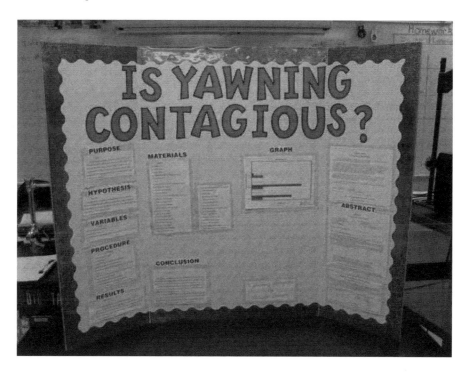

The Materials List needs to be before the procedure. The graph needs to be before the Results. The board is easy to follow and the title is catchy. See how the metallic border at the top of the board reflects the light? It is distracting.

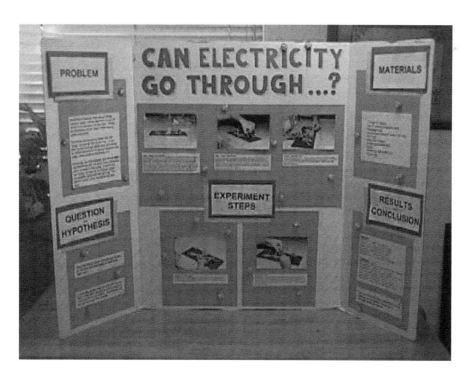

The pins that hold the paper onto the board are distracting. Otherwise, it is well organized and has a curiosity title.

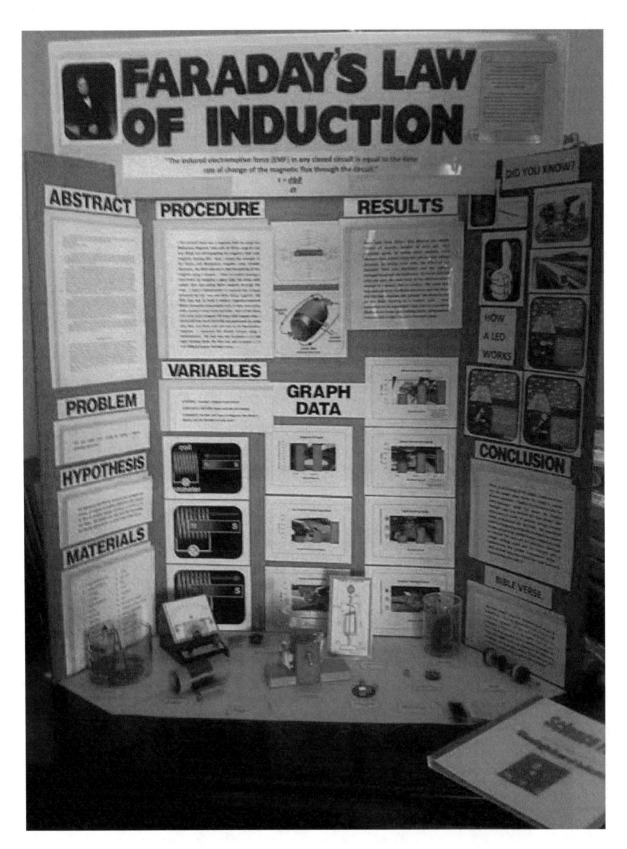

This looks like an Engineering project. Engineering projects do not have a hypothesis or variables.

This is a very clever board. The student used 5 colors (blue, red, gold, white and black). The border around the whole board pulls everything together. There are too many border colors around the sections of the papers (abstract, procedure, data, etc.)

What do you think of this display board?

Love this board. The student stayed with 3 colors. The header is clever. The notebook covers on the table match the borders on the board. It is well organized and easy to follow the headings.

What do you think of this board? Different way of displaying the results.

Some more clever ideas here.

Science Fairs

Why Enter a Science Fair?

There are so many reasons to enter a science fair, but the only reason to do so is because you want to or because your school requires you to enter. It is a huge commitment and you are probably already packed with activities, homework and family responsibilities.

The following is a list of benefits. See if one or more grabs your interests and motivates you to move forward.

1. Do you want to go to college?
    a. Colleges love to see that you're passionate about learning. If science or math is one of your favorite subjects, then this is an opportunity to showcase what you love and distinguish yourself on your college application.

    b. Some science fair sponsors offer monetary awards as well as scholarships. Will the cost of entering science fairs be outweighed by the possibility of winning a prize? Discuss this with your parents so you can set a budget. What can you contribute to the expenses?

2. A science fair project follows a step-by-step process as detailed in this book. Most students first do a project for their school science fair. Others also enter that same project at city or county level fairs and then go on to international competitions. Prizes can total over $3,000,000 and the top winners can take home up to $50,000 scholarships.

3. The process of doing a science fair project is actually a metaphor for what you will do every day in life when you make decisions. You make an educated guess about an outcome, take action to see if it works, then decide what to do after your experiment gives you feedback (results).

4. Doing a science fair project is a wonderful learning experience because it goes beyond science.
    a. For your research paper you will do investigative research and most likely complete the longest paper you've ever written.

    b. For the first time you will learn about the importance of a bibliography and how to write one.

    c. You will learn advanced computer research skills, office programs such as word processors and spreadsheets.

    d. Advance math skills will be used to collect and report data.

e. Various forms of communication will be used when you write your project report, design your display board and present your findings to your teacher, fellow students and the Judges at the fair.

f. You will learn advance communication skills as you proceed to bigger fairs and international fairs. As you move through the process you will hone your presentation skills so you can impress the Judges. These influential skills will be used throughout your career in whatever job or business you pursue.

5. Whether you are a middle school or high school student you will complete the longest assignment than any you have done. This project will probably take one to three months. It will require that you learn and implement planning and schedule strategies. There is no wiggle room for procrastination. These strategies will greatly benefit you during college and your career.

6. You will learn to be a more ethical person. Living in your word and being honest is all part of having integrity. Plagiarism, falsification of data, or exaggeration of your results must not be used.

7. You will learn how to be a more discerning person. When reading the newspaper, a journal or listening to the news, you will be more alert to false information and exaggerations. You will be able to make better decisions about most aspects of your life as health, friendship, jobs, etc.

Hope I did not scare you from doing a science fair project. Being armed with the truth will prepare you. The best you can do is to do a project about something that excites you and will keep you interested for the duration. Stay focused, stick to a daily plan by having a timeline, and be truthful for the duration.

What Science Fairs Look Like

Big / Top Fairs

IJAS – Illinois Junior Academy of Science

Intel ISEF

Science Fair Directory

How to Find Science Fairs and Other STEM / STEAM Competitions

There are hundreds of science fairs, engineering fairs, and other STEM competitions held locally, nationally, and internationally every year. Some competitions require students to start at the local level and win in their category to advance to the next level. Other competitions are open to all students. The listings below include both.

Featured STEM Competitions

Affiliated fairs are members of the **Society for Science & the Public network.** These competitions exist in nearly every state in the U.S. as well as over 70 other countries, regions and territories. Fairs are conducted at local, regional, state and national levels and can be affiliated with the Intel International Science and Engineering Fair (Intel ISEF) and/or the Broadcom MASTERS.

The **Intel ISEF** is an international pre-college science competition that provides an annual forum for over 1,700 young scientists, engineers and mathematicians from across the world to compete for approximately $4 million in awards. Students in grades 9-12 or equivalent must compete in an Intel ISEF affiliated science fairs around the world and win the right to attend the Intel ISEF. Each affiliated fair may send a predetermined number of projects to the Intel ISEF. Competition begins at the high school level and culminates at the International Science and Engineering Fair, which is usually held in May.

Broadcom MASTERS (Math, Applied Science, Technology and Engineering for Rising Stars) is the premier national science and engineering competition for U.S. middle school students (6th– 8th grade). It aims to encourage engineering and innovation amongst younger students. Society affiliated science fairs around the country nominate the top 10% of 6th, 7th and 8th grade participants to enter this prestigious competition. After submitting the online application, 300 semifinalists are chosen and 30 finalists present their research projects and compete for cash prizes in team hands-on STEM challenges to demonstrate their talents in critical thinking, collaboration, communication and creativity.

Broadcom MASTERS International is a global program that provides 20 middle school students with unique STEM learning experiences. To qualify, students must be nominated from regional fairs.

Fluor Engineering Challenge is an annual K-12 engineering challenge open to students in the U.S. and around the world. The goal is to inspire all students to try their hand at engineering. Materials are low-cost, and the time commitment is short. Participating schools and non-profit organizations are entered in a lottery for cash prizes.

Junior Solar Sprint is an annual model solar car building competition for 5th–8th grade U.S. students. Regional winners go on to compete nationally for prizes.

California Invention Convention is open to K-12 students in California, this competition has students invent their own product, process, or solution to a problem. Local school competitions lead to a state-wide final with prizes.

More Science Fairs, Engineering Fairs and STEM/STEAM Competitions
Conrad Foundation's Spirit of Innovation Challenge is an annual, multi-phase innovation and entrepreneurial competition that aims to attract young innovators and entrepreneurs around the world. It encourages collaborative work with the mission to develop innovative and viable scientific solutions to benefit the world. It challenges high school student teams (age 13-18) to solve real world problems in the areas of Aerospace Exploration & Aviation, Clean Energy & Environment, Cyber Technology & Security, and Health & Nutrition. For students age 13-18. A winning team is awarded $5000 to continue product development. Spirit of Innovation Awards are sponsored, in part, by Lockheed Martin Corporation.

Prize: Seed funding grants, investment opportunities, patent support, business services, scholarships and other opportunities to grow their solution into a real business.

Davidson Fellows Scholarship Program aims to recognize exceptional students and support them in the fulfillment of their potential. It includes categories of science, mathematics, and technology, among others. The top prize is $50,000.

Discovery Young Scientist Challenge (DYSC) is for students in grades 5-8. Ten finalists will receive $1,000 and an all-expenses-paid trip to St. Paul, MN for the competition finals. The first-place winner will receive $25,000.

International BioGENEius Challenge is for high school students only; recognizes outstanding research in biotechnology. Process is state, national, international; hosted by the Biotechnology Institute. Top prize is cash award is in the high 5 figures.

Team America Rocketry Challenge (TARC) is the world's largest model rocket contest, accepts teams of students in grades 7–12 from any U.S. school or non-profit youth organization.

The Junior Science and Humanities Symposia (JSHS) invites high school students in grades 9–12 to conduct an original research investigation in the sciences, engineering, or mathematics, and to participate in a regional symposium sponsored by universities or other academic institutions. Regional winners proceed to a national competition.

18 Biggest Science Fairs in the World

Local Science Fairs and More....
The **WWW Virtual Library Science Fairs Directory** lists Fairs Across the Nation and the World. This Library page is an attempt to provide a single comprehensive list of every science fair accessible through the World Wide Web, whether of global or local scope. Most science fairs in the U.S. and U.S. territories are held from January through March. Fairs outside the U.S. may take place at other times of the year. Students who participate in these fairs must observe the International Rules for Pre-college Science Research.

Regeneron Science Talent Search - **MIT THINK Scholars Program** is an MIT-led competition promoting STEM (science, technology, engineering and mathematics); it supports and funds projects developed by high school students. Organized by a group of undergraduates at MIT, THINK reaches out to students who have done extensive research on the background of a potential research project and are looking for additional guidance in the early stages of their project. Finalists receive all-expenses paid trips to MIT to attend xFair (MIT's spring tech symposium) and winners receive funding to build their projects.

Maker Faire Maker Faire Bay Area and World Maker Faire New York is an event open to participation by school students, for it is an all-ages gathering of like-minded 'making enthusiasts'; be it tech lovers, crafters, educators, tinkerers, hobbyists, engineers, science clubs, authors, artists, students or commercial exhibitors. Aimed at celebrating arts, crafts, engineering, science projects and the Do-It-Yourself (DIY) mindset, the Faire is an event created by Make: magazine. 'Mini' and 'Featured' are the two types of Faires and both varieties are independently organized but licensed by Maker Media; several editions of both have taken place across the world with the flagship Faires held in Bay Area and New York.
Prize: Increased exposure, experience and engagement with the Maker Faire Education Community which in turn encourages innovation.

Young Scientist Challenge is an engineering competition for young innovators. Students in grades 5-8 are eligible to compete. They are encouraged to provide novel solutions to help solve everyday problems in a 1 to 2-minute video. Winners receive $25,000, and finalists get to work one-on-one with some of 3M's top scientists and engineers. Finalists are announced in June/July and receive an exciting summer of mentoring before the grand prize winner is chosen in October.

RoboRAVE International is an open platform, international technology robotics competition. It is ideal for school students. It can feature any robot, using any software and any participant. Eligible teams comprise two to four players, one robot and one coach. The participants can be from elementary, middle or high school students and even Big Kids (which includes University students, teachers, engineers, hobbyists, etc.). Those up to the challenge could compete in a higher division, but they can't take part in multiple divisions of the same challenge.

Challenges vary from building and programming robots that can do the following: complete mazes, climb steep inclined planes, light and extinguish fire without contact, exhibit innovation, win at jousting/ sumo and carry out various tasks despite weighing less than an air vehicle. RoboEthics is a platform where opposing arguments are used to address the ethics of robotics in a global society.

Best Kept Secrets of How to Succeed at

The Science Fair

Using the Scientific Method

Madeline Binder, M.S.Ed. M.S. Human Services Counseling

Best Kept Secrets of How to Succeed at the Science Fair

Creating a winning science fair project is not magic. Like science itself, it is the result of following a *system* and working step by step to achieve a great result. You are just as capable of producing a winning project as the students who have won science fairs in the past.

Success at a science fair comes to those who have ideas and the discipline to implement them consistently. But doing this does not have to be painstaking, tedious, or ultra-intense. Indeed, it can be fun, engaging, and fascinating – so that you do not even feel any discomfort while you create your science fair project.

This checklist will help get you started on the exciting journey of designing a science fair project from the ground up. Print it out, keep it handy, and check the box next to each idea after you have put it into practice. Once you're finished with this checklist, you will be well on your way toward high honors at the science fair as well as having a wonderful learning experience!

Attitude with Quantum Physics
☐ **Have a positive attitude.**

Attitude is everything! Did you know that attitude determines the health of your cells? Yep!!!!

What is in your *mind* is the foremost determinant of the way you will experience reality. The attitude with which you approach your science fair project can make the difference between achieving honors and a poor performance.

By maintaining an upbeat, positive attitude, you can make it easier to shape the world around you as you create a winning project.

The science of quantum physics reveals how much in the external world depends on *us,* the observers. Indeed, many quantum scientists believe that the position of a subatomic particle is not determined until we look at it. Once we do the subatomic particle transitions from one of many *potential* states into the one *actual* state in which we perceive it – all because of us!

This is not just true of subatomic particles. Quantum physics tells us that humans have the ability to make choices out of infinite possible *potential* future states. We can make the particles follow one course. Human choices determine the outcome of human actions, and human *attitudes* determine human choices.

Also, our attitude produces feelings in our body. And those feelings produce energy. The "attitude energy" operates at different frequencies. And you attract into your life the people and events that are operating on the same frequency as you. This just about freaked me out when I learned this.

So now I check my attitude and change it if it is not supporting me in a positive way. What is your attitude at this moment?

How do you change your attitude? All energy is produced by pictures that we make in our head, consciously or unconsciously. Change your picture and you change your attitude.

Try this: visualize in your head a beautiful place that you have visited or seen in your travels. Is it a mirror lake? An awesome sunset? The black beaches of Hawaii?

Now notice the changes in your body. Notice how you feel. Do this every day when you wake up in the morning and before you go to bed... for 21 days. Then, let me know what happens in your life.

Your attitude is the place to start. Firmly *believe* that you can create a winning science fair project and the experience of doing so will be fun, rewarding, and informative.

Immerse yourself in a fascinating world of knowledge, and you can grow as a human being. This project doesn't have to consist of drudgery. Your attitude will determine whether it's a chore or a wonderful opportunity!

For an excellent resource about quantum mechanics and about how great an impact your *thoughts* can have on your life and on the world around you, check out the film, *What the Bleep Do We Know?* I think you can stream it for free on Amazon.com. It will challenge your mind, get it thinking in new ways, and get you into the right attitudinal frame to start on your project!

So laugh. Have fun. And enjoy the process.

Strategies for Success
☐ **Start early**.

Trust me! You do not want this to be you! And don't ask your parents to help you the last minute because you procrastinated... take charge of your project. Be responsible. This is your project – not theirs.

Typically, you will be given the directions for a science fair project about two to three months in advance. There are several reasons for this; your teacher knows that it takes that long to complete a science fair project and you will have an edge by starting early.

Yes, a science fair project takes a lot of work. Determining what you want to research, doing the research, designing an experiment, writing a detailed report, and preparing a creative, informative presentation cannot be done overnight.

Even if you try to do it in one or two weeks, you will feel incredibly rushed, and the work will cut into your other commitments and will force you to live an extremely uncomfortable schedule. Maybe even panic!

But, fortunately, by giving you the instructions early, your teacher is trying his/her best to help you avoid this problem. Working on a science fair project over the course of a few months not only enables you to do a better job; it also makes the work far *easier* and a lot *less stressful.*

Would you rather spend an hour every day working calmly, gradually, steadily at completing your science fair project – or would you rather cram in the work for eight hours a day in the last week before the project is due – losing sleep, becoming irritable, and having no time for relaxation, meeting with friends, finishing other assignments, or playing games? Starting your science fair project early makes your life a lot easier.

When you get a head start you can actually afford to delve into the material you're working with and find many *interesting* things about it, rather than simply trying to get everything done as fast as possible in an effort to race against time and meet the deadline.

As soon as you get your science fair project instructions, do something each day to move your project further toward completion.

Your daily contribution does not have to be enormous or time-consuming. Just spend thirty minutes to an hour per day doing some kind of work for the project – and you will be surprised at how quickly the results accumulate.

Remember what Anthony Robbins says: "Small step-by-step actions, consistently taken over a period of time, have a giant impact."

A poster can lift your spirits and supports a positive attitude. When my son was in high school, he put his posters and pictures above his bed on the ceiling. Every morning when he woke up, and before he went to bed, he did his visualization exercise.

☐ Choose a subject that interests you and holds your attention.
One of the most effective ways to make sure that you work regularly on your science fair project is to do an experiment about something that interests you.

If you are not naturally fascinated by certain scientific ideas or observations about the world around you, then complete this sentence, "I have always wondered about…."

A science fair project can be your chance to delve into subjects which already trigger your curiosity.

 Sit back and think about questions you are curious about or about areas of science that hold the most appeal for you.

You do not have to force yourself to work with an idea that does not interest you.

By choosing one that you enjoy you will be able to easily radiate *genuine enthusiasm* when the judges ask you questions. Remember, enthusiasm is contagious!

☐ Get Ideas From Others
Talk with your friends. Look at what has been done in previous years.

☐ Choose a highly specific question to investigate.
One crucial insight that many students miss is that *the more specific you write your scientific question, the less work you'll have to do.* This is another secret to producing an outstanding science fair project.

Some topic areas are so broad that investigating the entire topic area for your project is virtually impossible. For instance, not even the most talented, industrious, and interested student could pull off a science fair project on "biology," because biology is such a broad field that it occupies the life's work of millions of the best minds throughout the world!

But if you decide to do your project on some narrower *aspect* of biology and then ask a highly targeted question about that one aspect, you will be undertaking a much more reasonable task.

Try to narrow your project's purpose to something concrete. Instead of looking at a large *class* of events or things, make your science project about some particular *kind* of thing. If you're testing the wind turbine blades, it would be extremely difficult to conduct a project that tests *all* kinds of blades. But focusing on just 2 different materials used to make the blades is quite reasonable and will actually make for a superior project.

Science as a process relies on conducting precise experiments on specific objects. This means that it's far easier to do a science fair project if you're trying to analyze specific objects as opposed to generalities.

Furthermore, the conclusions you make about specific objects are far more likely to be reliable – because you'll be making fewer assumptions that might or might not hold true than when drawing general conclusions.

Once you have a general topic area which you would like to delve into, think of ways in which to narrow the specific problem your science project will explore. The narrower you can make it, the more focused and streamlined your project will be – translating into less work and better results.

☐ **Create a Timeline for Working on Your Project**
A science fair project is a large, multi-step, complex undertaking. It has many more components than anybody's mind can focus on at the same time. When students approach it as a single indivisible thing, it's no wonder that a science fair project can seem so daunting!

The key to successfully creating a science fair project is to mentally *divide it* into small, easily manageable steps. If you have gotten off to a head start on your project as advised in this checklist, then you can afford to complete a small, pre-determined part of your project.

Use the timeline in the Student's Appendix. You can also create one on your computer. Make a file and type in the dates every day between now and the science fair. Under each day, set an outcome that you would like to accomplish on your project. Make the goal extremely specific, so that you can easily determine whether it has been met or not.

A great idea for keeping you committed to your timeline is to insert a checklist box symbol next to each day. Go into the "Insert" menu in Microsoft Word, select the

"Symbol" option, and then the "Wingdings" font. You'll find a box symbol just like the one used for this checklist.

Then print out your timeline and post it in a highly visible location in your bedroom. Another good place is on your bedroom door so when you enter the room you see the timeline. Each day as you complete the task designated on the timeline, put a check mark in the corresponding box. This will be an excellent motivator every day because you will be able to observe the progress you've made and the day's contribution to it.

By the way, there is nothing preventing you from *working ahead* of your timeline. If you can do your project faster than you initially planned, then that will make for even less stress and more leisure immediately before the science fair. Use the timeline as a minimum baseline for what you need to do, but feel free to exceed your own expectations!

☐ **Make sure your project idea meets the requirements of good scientific research**. A good scientific research project involves a test of something where the results can be guessed, but are not known for certain. You find out whether your educated guess is accurate by doing an experiment. The purpose of a science project is to discover something new.

Is there something that could be changed to help answer the question?
Change only one thing (called a variable) in the experiment.

Find out how you can make the change happen.

Search for a method that will tell how the amount of change can be measured.
Plan for a "control group" that is not changed so that the change can be observed.

Simple experiments are best. If the experiment is too complex, unknown variables can interfere with the results.

Even if your experiment does not work, or something unexpected happens, you will have learned something. Sometimes unsuccessful scientific research is used as a model for other experiments. Knowing that something did not work is actually knowing a lot.

Scientists often study very complex problems. They can spend a lifetime and not find the answers. Even so, their research is valuable to other scientists. The failed experiment can be used by someone to find out an answer. Are you that someone?

Steps in Creating Your Project Checklist
☐ **State the purpose of the project**.
What do you want to find out? Write a statement describing what you want to do. Use your observations and questions to write the statement.

☐ **Craft a hypothesis.**
Make a list of answers to the questions you have. This can be a list of statements describing how or why you think the subject of your experiment works. The hypothesis must be stated so that it can be tested by an experiment.

☐ **Design an experimental procedure to test the hypothesis.**
Design an experiment to test each hypothesis. Make a step-by-step list of what you will do to address the hypothesis. This list is called an experimental procedure.

☐ **Obtain materials and equipment.**
Make a list of items you need in order to do the experiment and prepare the items. Try to use every day, household items. If you need special equipment, ask your teacher for assistance. Local colleges or businesses might be able to loan materials to you.

You must also determine what equipment, supplies or materials are necessary to complete the study. Prior to conducting an experiment, it is important to document data collection methods. This step will ensure the quality of the experiment if someone else should reproduce it.

☐ **Collect data.**
In order to test your hypothesis, data must be collected. You must design a plan that considers: *what to collect? When to collect? Where to collect? How many samples are necessary?*

Developing sample surveys involves determining appropriate sample size, monitoring frequency and the need for repetition. Through the use of variables and controls, results can be determined and documented.

Variables are those factors being tested in an experiment that are usually compared to a control. **A control** is a known measure to which scientists can compare their results.

Most scientific papers published in journals include a method's section documenting the way in which the experiment was performed. Attention must be paid to make sure that data collection methods are kept unbiased.

Data can be represented by many formats.

Data can be defined as a single piece of information such as names; dates or values made from observations. Data is used daily at scientific institutions and government agencies (e.g., EPA and USFWS). Datasets are one or more associated data values, which can be used to test a scientific theory. When conducting an experiment, it is also important to record all measurements, even if they don't seem correct.

☐ **Analyze the data.**
This step is necessary to prove or disprove a hypothesis by experimentation. The methods involved in testing/analyzing the data are also important since an experiment must be able to be repeated by others to ensure the quality of results.

For instance, if two people on different sides of the country decide to perform the same experiment, they must end up with the same results. Statistics are then used to analyze the data. Descriptive statistics are a means of summarizing observational data through the calculation of a mean, mode, average, standard deviation, variance, etc.

☐ Summarize your results and draw conclusions.
The presentation of the results is very important. Often scientists will rely heavily on graphics, tables, flow charts, maps and diagrams to facilitate the interpretation of the results. Graphics can be used to model future predictions.

Graphics like scatter plots can also assist with the identification of relationships (correlations) between two parameters. If two variables are correlated, when one changes, the other will do so in a related manner. This relationship can be either positive or negative.

Often when a correlation is found, it is assumed that there is a "cause and effect" relationship between the variables. Although there needs to be some logical basis for relating variables, cause is not demonstrated with a statistical technique.

When we say two variables are correlated, we can say that they are associated in some way. A written discussion documenting identifiable trends or correlations generally accompanies these graphics. This step is just the presentation of results; it does not include any interpretation.

☐ Discuss the experiment's limitations and your conclusions.
This is the section where the hypothesis is accepted or rejected. Many scientists no longer try to define cause and affect parameters, but instead identify relationships between the data. In this manner, ideas can be formed about why certain results were found while identifying previous studies that may have had similar or contradicting results.

It is important to reference all studies you used so that other scientists and science fair judges can refer to them if necessary.

☐ Identify future research needs.
This may include areas of related interest that need to be studied to better understand the subject. This section can also give information about limitations of the study, such as what items should be modified to try to reach the intended goal.

How to Stand Out Above the Crowd
☐ Be fresh!
Judges always look for original ideas. Original projects are those that take what you read about in textbooks or on the Internet and take them one step further by exploring new ground and innovative techniques.

☐ **Be clear and direct in order to impress the judges**.
You may have a super idea for a project but it won't impress the judges (or teacher) if you don't have a well-defined goal or objective. Be very specific about what solution you want to solve or improve upon?

A direct, often simple objective won't leave the judges scratching their heads, trying to figure out what exactly you were want to prove. You've got to pass the "HUH?" test.

☐ **Make sure you understand your own project in depth**.
You must show the judges that YOU understand and know how to use scientific theory, terms, techniques and methodologies. Judges look for students who know about the scientific principles and practices they used in their project. They want to see if you can interpret and apply what you learned.

It's important for judges to know that you have a depth of understanding of the basic science behind the project, that you comprehend the process. That you're aware of any influence or affects the project has on related subject topics. If you don't know what a term or theory means… find out or don't use it in your presentation.
Keep your project at a level YOU can understand. Judges aren't expecting you to have access to university research laboratories or be a Ph.D. candidate. What is important is that the technical level of sophistication and complexity of your project reflect YOUR level of understanding – not someone else's. It's OK to receive help outside your school as long as you clearly say what kind of help you received and who specifically helped you.

IF YOU DON'T UNDERSTAND IT, DON'T DO IT, because you won't be able to explain it! Chances are if it doesn't make sense to you, it won't make sense to the judge.

One more thing… know how all your equipment works, what it does and why it was used in your project. If you can't explain it to a judge, then s/he will probably not understand the science behind your experiment.

☐ **Provide all the evidence for the claims you make**.
Judges look for complete projects. That is, projects that are thorough in addressing the original question and thorough in answering other questions that come up during the experimentation process. As a scientist, it is your responsibility to provide all evidence to support whatever claims you are making. It isn't up to the judge or other scientists to prove your claim.

Without data or results that support your claims, it's not a completed work.

Tips for a Great Display
☐ Check with your teacher to see if your school has any specific guidelines on the size, style or shape of the display.

☐ Keep the display simple – include only the essentials.

☐ Let the headlines tell the story – no lengthy descriptions.

☐ Check your spelling.

☐ When possible, use color to clarify information (charts, diagrams and graphs).

☐ Use photographs or drawings to help show what was done.

☐ Make the display as neat as possible. If you have access to a computer to make charts, graphs, and labels – that's fine. If you don't, you can still make an attractive, neat, and effective display. Use a stencil and ruler if possible. If you have to use a pencil, carefully go over the pencil lines with a dark marker.

☐ Let the teacher or science fair chairperson know early if the display needs electricity or other special arrangements.

☐ Use safe, durable materials. Make sure everything used in the display meets school safety standards.

Questions to be Prepared For
Judges will ask lots of questions about your project. Dazzle them with your brilliance and be prepared to answer questions like these.

☐ **Make sure you can respond to each of these questions**.
How did you come up with the idea for this project?

What did you learn from your background research?

How did you design you experiment?

How much time (or many days) did it take to run the experiments or collect each data point?

How many times did you run the experiment with a different set of parameters?

Did you try something else that didn't work?

Can you explain to me how your project relates to some scientific principle?

Were there any references that helped you do your analysis?

When did you start this project? Or how much of the work did you do this year?

What is the next experiment you would like to do to continue this study?

Day of the Science Fair
Dress for Success
Celebrate after the Science Fair

PARENT'S APPENDIX

Information on the Scientific Method
All science fair projects include the six steps of the scientific method. See the chart, *How to Help at Each Step* which is included in this guide.

Time Management
Help your child complete the tasks assigned by allowing time to go to the public library and to work with his/her team. If there is a conflict with family vacation and events, please contact the teacher so s/he can work something out and still keep your child on track.

How to Help Your Child
This is probably the longest and most intense project your child will take on in the elementary grades or high school. With other school and family obligations, even the best student can get overwhelmed, or hit a "roadblock" and lose the ability to stay on track or even finish their project. The fun and creativity come to a halt.

Enthusiastic patience is the key without *saving* your child instead of stepping in and doing his / her project.

Science Fairs are annual events where students are encouraged to carry out scientific investigations. At some science fairs, students also compete for various levels of recognition.

Whether or not your children win recognition or go on to a regional, state or national competition is not the focus. What is important is that your children believe in their greatness by experiencing small successes during the journey.

It is in the *practice of science* that they learn to approach life's challenges in a systematic way. This is what this event is really all about.

In What Modality Does Your Child Learn?
This is probably the longest and most intense project your child will take on in the elementary grades or high school. With other school and family obligations the best student can get overwhelmed, hit a "roadblock" and cannot seem to stay on track or even finish their project. Fun and creativity come to a halt.

Sometimes getting stuck means your child needs to discover how s/he learns best. Find out what to do to help your child stay focused on a task, and much more! I took this test myself. It was right on target. Take an online learning profile which will give in-depth information to your child's style of learning. (https://tinyurl.com/yf2bpya9)

Safety Guidelines:
Society for Science.org (https://tinyurl.com/yzkzrs52)

Information
I am not an attorney, so I am not offering legal advice, just want to raise awareness. If your child does an original science fair project that you believe can make money on the open market, or before your child becomes involved with a hospital, pharmaceutical company or business who may want to pay for their research, suggest you contact a legal professional.

There are non-profit groups that will give you with legal advice. A family attorney or your local Chamber of Commerce can lead you in the right direction. If you live near a law school, most of them have Clinics. Here law students work under the supervision of a professor. Some clinics are free and others charge a minimal price.

How Parents Can Help at Each Step

Project Step	How to Help	Do Not....
Step 1. **Ask a Question**	Discussing with your child whether a project idea is practical. Network and give names of experts to interview.	Pick an idea and project for your child. Your child needs to choose their own project so they stay excited. S/he must own this project.
Step 2. **Doing background research**	Be your child's chauffeur. Transport him / her to and from the library. You can help your child think of keywords by asking "what" questions. "*What words do you think will lead you to information on this topic?*"	Do keyword or Internet search. Print the articles and links.
Step 3. **Write a hypothesis**	Ask how the hypothesis relates to the experiment the child wants to do.	Write the hypothesis yourself.
Step 4. **Test the hypothesis by doing the experiment.**	Assist finding supplies and materials. Monitor safety. Only help to build something if your child asks for help. Only help with unsafe steps.	Write the experiment procedure. Do the experiment. Tell the child what to do.
Step 5. **Analyzing data and drawing conclusions**.	Ask your child, "What would be the best way to record the data?" You can remind your child that the data needs to tie back to the hypothesis and used when drawing conclusions.	Create the spreadsheet. Make the graphs & tables. State the conclusion.
Step 6. **Communicate results.**	Allow your child to write his/own report alone! When practicing his presentation for the judges be an enthusiastic member of the audience. Display board: Transportation expert!	Hands off materials, supplies and the display board! Do not mention ideas for color scheme or placement of graphs, table, data or objects.

Be an Admirer

Author's Message

Hi!

This book is an accumulation of my journey as an educator and human services counselor. The information has evolved over the years, taking into account the changes due to COVID and the advancement in technology. I have to admit that I poured my heart into every thought that went on each page.

I am really interested in knowing how this book was helpful to you. If there is anything that you think I need to do to improve this guide, let me know that too. Would love your comments and feedback. You can reach me through my email:
mdbinder1942@gmail.com

Feel free to tell me if you found any errors, need more information, or just to say hello.

Thank you for using this book.

Cheers!
Madeline Binder

Made in the USA
Monee, IL
11 September 2024

78f71535-c591-4935-bf5a-79caadd12ae3R01